*TWAYNE'S WORLD AUTHORS SERIES*
*A Survey of the World's Literature*

# CHINA

William Schultz, University of Arizona

EDITOR

Tung  Yüeh

TWAS 498

序。日出三界則情根盡離聲
聞緣覺則妄想空又曰出
三界不越三界離聲聾緣
覺不越聲聞緣覺一念着

First page of *Hsi-yu pu* preface

# TUNG YÜEH

### By FREDERICK P. BRANDAUER
*University of Washington*

## TWAYNE PUBLISHERS
A DIVISION OF G. K. HALL & CO., BOSTON

Copyright © 1978 by G. K. Hall & Co.

Published in 1978 by Twayne Publishers,
A Division of G. K. Hall & Co.
All Rights Reserved

Printed on permanent/durable acid-free paper and bound
in the United State of America

*First Printing*

**Library of Congress Cataloging in Publication Data**

Brandauer, Frederick P
Tung Yüeh.
(Twayne's world authors series ; TWAS 498 : China)
Bibliography: p. 169–173
Includes index.
1. Tung, Yüeh, 1620–1686.   Hsi yu pu.
2. Tung, yüeh, 1620–1686.   3. Authors, Chinese—Biography. I.
Title.
PL2698.T83H733        895.1'3'4        78-19058
ISBN 0–8057–6339–2

To Millie

# *Contents*

# About the Author

The son of missionaries, Frederick P. Brandauer was raised in China and later himself served for eight years in Hongkong under the United Methodist Church. In 1973 he completed a doctoral program in Chinese literature at Stanford University and has since then been Assistant Professor of Chinese at the University of Washington, Seattle. Professor Brandauer has published articles and translations on Chinese literature and Chinese religion and is co-author of the book, *Folk Religion in an Urban Setting: A Study of Hakka Villagers in Transition.*

# *Preface*

This book offers two things: a short biography of an obscure but important seventeenth-century Chinese author named Tung Yüeh and an in-depth critical study of the *Hsi-yu pu,* the work by which he is best known in Chinese literature. Although in terms of length and volume of material the emphasis is definitely on the latter, the organization adopted reflects this dual purpose. Since the *Hsi-yu pu* is a vernacular novel, this book may be read either as a general, concise, and factual presentation of the life of one Chinese author or as a work in literary criticism of one example of traditional Chinese fiction. Hopefully the book will be read as both with the recognition that in literature, biography and criticism rightfully go together. In any case, the assumption behind the writing of this book is that an adequate understanding of the importance of an author requires an informed appreciation of the specific literary merits of his work.

Following an introductory chapter which contains necessary background information, the main body of this book is presented in two parts. What I have attempted to do in the biographical chapters is to introduce Tung Yüeh, the man. Chapter 2 gives the basic facts one would expect to find in a biography under three subdivisions of his ancestry, the main events of his life, and his writings. Chapter 3 moves from basic facts to interpretation and focuses on Tung Yüeh's personality and activities with particular attention given to Liu Fu's charge that Tung was mentally ill, Tung's political involvements, and finally his relationship to Buddhism. This third chapter serves as a direct link with the critical study, for it provides background materials on Tung's temperament, inclinations, interests, and experiences which are important for an adequate understanding of his novel.

In the critical study of Tung Yüeh's *Hsi-yu pu* I have attempted to introduce the literary skill and artistic achievements of Tung Yüeh, the author. Three chapters are devoted to the materials in the novel and three to the world of the novel. The materials are seen as verbal materials (language), narrative materials (story), and conceptual materials (theme). There is, of course, an overlapping of these in many parts and sometimes it has been difficult to separate them. For instance, the story and the theme run together in the beginning and concluding sections of the novel. Also all three types of materials support each other. The story and the theme reinforce each other and, of course, both are dependent on the language.

In spite of this interweaving and interdependence of function, the materials are of three distinct kinds and Chapters 4, 5, and 6 may be characterized as the analytic ones. These may be contrasted with Chapters 7, 8, and 9 which are the synthetic chapters wherein the world of the *Hsi-yu pu* is shown to be projected at three separate levels. There is the world as dream in which Monkey, the main character, is simply a fictional dreamer and Tung Yüeh is presenting to us a study in psychological realism. There is the world as satire in which Monkey becomes someone who through the distortions of his dream faces certain distressing problems in late Ming society. Here Tung Yüeh offers the reader in very effective and often subtle form his own kind of social protest. Finally, there is the world as myth in which Monkey represents the collective experience of man, first more generally as universal man, and then in particular as man in late Ming China. At the level of myth Monkey becomes the archetypal hero of Joseph Campbell's monomyth and although in Tung's hands this becomes an example of its Buddhist version, it is monomyth all the same.

The relationship of the materials to the three levels of world is one of remarkable coherence in complexity. The relationship is analogous to that within a kaleidoscope between the many pieces of glass and the patterns formed. The materials remain the same; yet as the various levels of the world are considered, they shift and, as it were, form new patterns. For instance, there is the conceptual material which is central to the theme of the *Hsi-yu pu* that desire is the source of man's troubles. In the world as dream this becomes Monkey's personal desire which causes him to have a bad dream. In the world as satire it becomes the desire of man in Ming society which leads to all sorts of social evils. In the world as myth it becomes the desire of collective man which causes the great illusion which is human life itself.

In dealing with the world I have not suggested that there are three worlds but that there is one world perceived at three levels. The distinction is an important one, for all three levels are part of the total world of the novel. They must all be recognized if the full artistic purpose of Tung Yüeh is to be understood, evaluated, and appreciated.

I have not provided either a complete translation of the *Hsi-yu pu* or a synopsis of its contents. To offer a fully annotated translation requires the production of a separate volume and at the time of this writing a translation has already been completed by two competent scholars, Professor Lin Shuen-fu and Mr. Larry J. Schulz, and merely awaits publication. Those desiring an English synopsis may consult Robert E. Hegel's M.A. thesis which contains a short, highly useful chapter-by-chapter summary of the novel's contents.

My own interest in Tung Yüeh came initially by way of his *Hsi-yu pu*. It was while a student at the University of Pittsburgh more than ten years ago that I first came in contact with the literary tradition of the great Westward Journey and started to read Wu Ch'eng-en's famous *Hsi-yu chi*. Serious study of the tradition, however, was not begun until later, when at Stanford University, I took graduate courses in Chinese fiction. In this context I was introduced to Tung's supplement and when turning my attention in its direction soon found myself thoroughly fascinated first by this remarkable novel and then by its unusual author. If in the following pages I can share with the reader even a fraction of the immense pleasure and satisfaction I have gained through this study I shall have been amply rewarded for my efforts.

Portions of Chapters 8 and 9 have already appeared in the *Tamkang Review* and the *Journal of the American Oriental Society* (see the Selected Bibliography for references).

There are many teachers, friends, and family members to whom I owe thanks for advice and help. I want especially to express gratitude to Professors James J. Y. Liu, John C. Y. Wang, and William Lyell, all of Stanford University, for assistance at an earlier stage of this work. They saved me more often than I care to admit from serious misinterpretations and incorrect translations. During my years at Stanford I was fortunate to receive several government fellowships and grants making possible continuation of my study and it is with gratitude that I acknowledge this support. I wish also to express appreciation to the staff of the East Asia Collection of the Hoover Institution for assistance especially in locating and consulting local gazetteers. Despite much valuable and generous help received I alone am responsible for any faults and errors which may appear either in content, analysis, or style.

FREDERICK P. BRANDAUER

*University of Washington*

# Acknowledgments

Grateful acknowledgment is made of permission to quote from materials protected under copyright: to Cambridge University Press for permission to quote from The *Hsi-yu chi: A Study of Antecedents to the Sixteenth-Century Chinese Novel* by Glen Dudbridge; to the Free Press for permission to quote from *A Short History of Chinese Philosophy* by Fung Yu-lan; to Harcourt Brace Jovanovich, Inc. for permission to quote from *Theory of Literature* by René Wellek and Austin Warren and from *Modern Man in Search of a Soul* by C. G. Jung; to the New American Library for permission to quote from *The Religions of Man* by Huston Smith; to Oxford University Press for permission to quote from *The Nature of Narrative* by Robert Scholes and Robert Kellogg; to Princeton University Press for permission to quote from *The Hero with a Thousand Faces* by Joseph Campbell and from *The Anatomy of Satire* by Gilbert Highet; to the University of Chicago Press for permission to quote from *The Rhetoric of Fiction* by Wayne C. Booth and from *The Art of Chinese Poetry* by James J. Y. Liu; and to the University of Wisconsin Press for permission to quote from *Wen-lin: Studies in the Chinese Humanities* edited by Chow Tsetsung.

# Chronology

CHAPTER 1

# Introduction

## I Biographical Sources

IMPORTANT sources for the biographical study in Chapters 2 and 3 may conveniently be classified into three kinds. Although we have extant today what appears to be only a small fraction of what Tung Yüeh wrote, yet this is substantial in volume and especially useful for his biographer. In the preface to his *Feng-ts'ao An ch'ien-chi (Former Collection from Abundant Grass Hermitage)* Tung wrote, "In reading books one should arrange by year,"[1] and he then proceeded to show how he had done just this in compiling various literary collections. Later in the preface he also wrote, "In writing books one should arrange by year."[2] Accordingly, he then presented a list of his own books, carefully giving the year in which each was written. A concern for accurate dating is reflected also in the diary Tung kept, part of which is still extant today.[3] In his collections of poetry and prose, Tung frequently added explanatory notes, often giving dates of composition and interesting background material. Unfortunately, a great many of Tung's works were deliberately destroyed and those which have survived cover only limited periods of his life and deal only with what must have been regarded in his day as politically innocuous subjects. Thus, they present a decidedly spotty and partial picture.

The local gazetteers for the areas associated with Tung's life also provide biographical source materials. For most of his life Tung lived and worked in the general region of Lake T'ai (T'ai Hu) in northern Chekiang and southern Kiangsu Provinces. His native place of Nan-hsün Township (Nan-hsün Chen) in northern Chekiang, not far from the southern shore of Lake T'ai, is remarkable for the large number of gazetteers it has generated.[4] Two of these have been of particular value, for in addition to other relevant materials they contain short biographies of Tung Yüeh.[5] Nan-hsün was a part of Wu-hsing County (Wu-hsing Hsien), which in turn was under the administrative jurisdiction of Hu-chou Prefecture (Hu-chou Fu). One of the gazetteers for this prefecture, also with a short biography, has been useful.[6] A gazetteer for the Lake T'ai area itself, one for Wu County (Wu Hsien) in Kiangsu Province which encompasses not only the eastern islands in Lake T'ai but also most of its eastern shore, and another one for Soochow Prefecture (Su-chou Fu) have also been consulted and have provided important information with geographical problems.[7]

Finally, there are what we might call private secondary sources. Chief among these are writings about Tung Yüeh, and here two twentieth-century studies are outstanding. The first and by far the longest is Liu Fu's "*Hsi-yu pu* tso-che Tung Jo-yü chuan" (Biography of Tung Jo-yü, Author of the *Hsi-yu pu*).[8] Liu Fu has painstakingly searched through most of the materials mentioned above and has culled from these passages relevant to Tung's life. The many quotations he supplies render his study a handy source of extensive and varied information, and although in this respect his work is indispensable, the major conclusions he draws regarding Tung's life are open to serious question. A second modern study is that by Hsü Fu-ming.[9] Hsü represents modern mainland scholarship and therefore his approach to Tung's life and the conclusions he draws regarding Tung's significance are altogether different from those of Liu Fu. In applying a Marxist analysis of history, Hsü is led to a narrowness of view which is also open to serious question.

## II   *The* Hsi-yu pu

Chapters 4 through 9 are a critical study of Tung Yüeh's best-known work, his novel the *Hsi-yu pu*. The three characters in the title are translated as "A Supplement to the *Westward Journey*,"[10] and as this shows, the novel is to be taken at least in part as a dependent one. What is supplemented is the famous novel *Hsi-yu chi (Record of the Westward Journey)*.[11] From the beginning of the *Hsi-yu pu* there is no doubt whatever regarding what is to be supplemented and where the supplement is to fit. In the very first prose passage of the first chapter reference is made to the T'ang Monk and his three disciples, who are said to have just left Flaming

Mountain (Huo-yen Shan).[12] The Monk is the famous Tripitaka and his disciples are Monkey, Pigsy, and Sandy, and these are the chief characters in the *Hsi-yu chi*.[13] In this earlier novel the Flaming Mountain episode appears in Chapters 59 through 61, and the supplement is thus intended to be inserted after this episode. The reader's familiarity with the earlier novel is assumed by the author.

In spite of its form as a supplement, the *Hsi-yu pu* is actually quite different from the *Hsi-yu chi,* and this is immediately apparent in the fact that fourteen of its sixteen chapters contain a long and involved dream sequence. The dream is Monkey's dream, in which he undergoes a succession of weird and often terrifying experiences. The dream takes the novel out of the realm of common reality and also out of the realm of reality in the *Hsi-yu chi*. It thus frees the author from the restrictions of the logic of our common understanding of wakeful reality and also of the logic of the reality of the realm of the *Hsi-yu chi* and allows him to make full use of his powers of imagination to explore a highly complex world. Thus, it is the dream which makes possible a complexity in the novel which includes psychological, religious, historical, social, political, and mythical elements.

### III   Hsi-yu pu *Authorship and Date*

Credit for the discovery of conclusive evidence for both the authorship and the date of the *Hsi-yu pu* must go to Liu Fu, and this evidence has been presented in his study of the life of Tung Yüeh, mentioned above. In Tung Yüeh's *Shih-chi* there is a group of poems in seven-syllable regulated-verse form under the collective title of "Man-hsing shih-shou" (Ten Poems of Random Inspirations). Liu Fu quotes the last two lines of the fourth poem, which read as follows:

The *Hsi-yu (Westward Journey)* has been supplemented with Yü Ch'u's pen,[14]
And the Wan-ching Lou (Tower of Myriad Mirrors) is empty upon the return of the successful candidate.[15]

A note added by Tung himself reads, "Ten years ago I supplemented the *Westward Journey* and it has one part on the Tower of Myriad Mirrors."[16] This set of poems is given among the larger group of poems dated in the cyclical year *keng-yin*, which refers to the seventh year of the Shun-chih reign, or 1650.[17]

One may raise the question as to whether or not Tung intended that the "ten years" be taken literally. There is no way to be certain about this. The earliest edition of the novel appears to have been published in 1641, and this suggests that the number of years between the time of writing and the 1650 date could not have been less than ten years. Of course, it could have been more than ten years, with "ten years" simply being used as a round number. However, the correspondence between the publication date of 1641 and the literal interpretation of the ten years of the poem, which places the date of writing at 1640, is so appropriate that with no evidence to the contrary it seems justified to assume that the novel was written or at least completed in 1640.

If we accept this date it means that the novel was written before the end of the Ming dynasty. It also means that it was written by Tung Yüeh when he was twenty years old. Actually both of these points reflect arguments used by those favoring a later dating of the novel. It has been argued that the novel contains anti-Ch'ing sentiment and that therefore it must have been written after 1644.[18] There are two problems with this argument. The first is that it is questionable whether or not there is clear anti-Ch'ing sentiment in the novel.[19] The second is that even if such sentiment can be demonstrated, it is not at all clear that this could not have been expressed prior to 1644.[20]

It has also been argued that the novel is the work of a matured thinker and writer and could not therefore have been written by a twenty-year-old.[21] This argument is equally problematic since Tung Yüeh appears to have been very gifted as a child,[22] and we also know that at about the age of twenty he was involved with the Fu She (Revival Society).[23] His high level of intellectual endowments, coupled with a manifest exposure to current problems and thought, would have been sufficient to make possible the writing of the novel at this early age. Both of the above arguments for a later date, however, become merely academic in the face of Liu Fu's evidence, and the dispute over authorship and date must be regarded as ended, at least until solid contrary evidence is provided.

## IV   Hsi-yu pu *Editions*

### A.   *The original 1641 edition.*

Found in a Peking library, this has now been reproduced by

photolithic process, first by the Wen-hsüeh Ku-chi K'an-hsing She in Peking in 1955 and then again by the Shih-chieh Shu-chü in Taipei in 1958.[24] Given by the modern editors as a wood-block edition from the Ch'ung-chen reign period,[25] it contains a preface dated in mid-autumn of the cyclical year *hsin-szu,* a date corresponding to the year 1641.[26] The preface is by a certain Yi-ju Chü-shih (Layman Yi-ju) at a place called Ch'ien-ch'ing Yün (Thousand-*ch'ing* Cloud),[27] and is significant chiefly because it applies a Buddhist interpretation to the novel and classifies the dream in the novel according to the traditional scheme found in the *Chou Li (Rites of Chou).*[28]

Following the preface are sixteen full-page wood-block pictures showing scenes from the novel. Striking in their detail and vividness even in the photolithic reprints, one can only imagine what the original prints must have looked like and how they must have enhanced the total artistic effect of the first edition.

Next comes a piece entitled "*Hsi-yu pu* ta-wen" (Replies to Questions on the *Hsi-yu pu*). An inscription at the end indicates that this was written by a certain Ching-hsiao Chai Chu-jen (Master of the Ching-hsiao Studio).[29] I am inclined to accept the view that this was in fact Tung Yüeh himself.[30] The Ching-hsiao Studio was one which belonged to Tung Yüeh's father, Tung Szu-chang. The father's collection of writings extant today appears in four *chüan* in the *Wu-hsing ts'ung-shu* under the title of *Ching-hsiao Chai yi-wen (Literary Remains from the Ching-hsiao Studio).*[31] We know that Tung Yüeh's father died when Tung Yüeh was just a young boy, and that Tung had no brothers.[32] Although I have not been able to discover other passages, apart from the novel, in which the title of Master of the Ching-hsiao Studio is used to refer to Tung Yüeh, it seems most likely that at the death of his father he would have been the one not only to inherit the studio but also to assume this title. Moreover, in this 1641 edition of the novel, the author of the main text is also said to be the Master of the Ching-hsiao Studio.[33] Clearly this now refers to Tung Yüeh. Finally, the second question in this piece reads as follows:

Question: In the old book of the *Westward Journey* there are a million spirits and demons and all they want to do is cut up the T'ang Monk and eat his flesh. Now you have supplemented the *Westward Journey* but the Mackerel only beguiles Monkey. Why is this?[34]

In the original the word which I have translated as the second person pronoun, "you," is *tzu,* which is the normal way the word is used in classical Chinese. The word could, however, refer to a third person and mean something like "the philosopher" (i.e., Tung Yüeh), but given the context this is unlikely. Thus, we seem to have here a question posed directly to the author of the novel by the author himself.

This particular essay takes on somewhat greater significance if, as we assume, it was written by Tung Yüeh. In reading it one might expect to find clues pointing to the author's purposes. Altogether, it contains twelve questions and their answers, which reflect a Buddhist interpretation of the novel and contain just what one would expect Tung to write, given the disturbed situation of the late Ming period. Anyone writing social or political protest would hardly announce that he was doing so. To do this would only be to invite disaster. Thus, Tung confines himself to a Buddhist interpretation, although the novel is far more than just a Buddhist story.

Following these preliminary materials is the main text, in sixteen chapters with occasional marginal notes and comments at the end of each chapter. As this edition appears to be the original one, I have used it for all translations and have only rarely deviated from its text.

B. *The Early Ch'ing* Shuo-k'u *Edition.*

This appears in the collectanea *Shuo-k'u*[35] and contains first a preface which ends with the words, "Written by T'ien-mu Shan-ch'iao in the first winter month of the year *kuei-ch'ou.*"[36] Reference is made here to a work called *Hsi-yu chen-ch'üan,* and thus the preface appears to be the same one mentioned by Liu Ts'un-yan in his report on Chinese popular fiction in two London libraries. Liu quotes the authorship and date given for this preface and then writes:

We do not know what this particular cyclical year was. However, the Preface refers to another novel, "The True Exposition of the Pilgrimage" (*Hsi-yu chen-ch'üan*). As the earliest edition of the latter work was one of 1780, this particular *kuei-ch'ou* must have been after that year, possibly 1793 (the 58th year of the Ch'ien-lung reign).[37]

Following the preface are the "Replies to Questions" appearing in the 1641 edition. A note at the end, however, indicates that these are not complete, and in comparing this text with the earlier edition we find that the last six characters of the twelfth and final answer are missing.[38]

After this comes the *"Hsi-yu pu* tsung-shih" (General Explanation of the *Hsi-yu pu*). A passage at the beginning of this essay indicates that the publisher of the edition was a certain Taoist named San-yi. Believing that readers would require further assistance in understanding the novel, he asked the writer, a certain Chen-k'ung Chü-shih (Layman Chen-k'ung), to provide a general explanation. What follows is a summary of the novel interspersed with explanatory comments. The basic framework for interpretation is the Taoist *yin-yang* theory of ascendance and decline. Various events in the novel are explained as resulting from either too much *yin* or too much *yang,* and progress throughout is controlled by an effort to balance the two. The "General Explanation" has special value for the modern student in that the writer also discusses various verbal devices, such as those which support the basic allegorical scheme.

Authorship for the text itself is ascribed to Tung Yüeh. Included with the text are frequent notes, which are in the form of commentary on the meaning of the novel. Little help is provided on strictly textual matters, however, and the position taken corresponds with that in the "General Explanation." This may indicate that both the notes and the "General Explanation" were written by the same Layman Chen-k'ung.[39]

Following the text is a final section called "Hsü *Hsi-yu pu* tsa-chi" (Additional Miscellaneous Notes on the *Hsi-yu pu*). In this essay both the *Hsü Hsi-yu (Sequel to the Westward Journey)* and the *Hou Hsi-yu (Later Westward Journey)* are mentioned. These are continuation novels in the *Hsi-yu* tradition, and since the latter one seems to have been written in the early Ch'ing period, the notes must have been written subsequent to this time.[40] No authorship is given for the notes. In content they present various discussions on questions related to the meaning of the novel, and again stress is placed on the Buddhist theme.

## C. *The 1958 Punctuated Edition.*

Published by the Hong Kong Commercial Press in 1958, this contains a fully punctuated text which makes it the most convenient edition to use. Included are the original preface by Layman Yi-ju, the "Replies to Questions" by the Master of Ching-hsiao Studio, and the "Miscellaneous Notes." Also Liu Fu's article is given as an appendix.

## V   *Theoretical Framework*

The theoretical framework for the critical study in Chapters 4 through 9 is essentially the one proposed by René Wellek and Austin Warren in their book *Theory of Literature.*[41] Wellek and Warren reject the old approach whereby a work of literary art was dichotomized into two parts, originally labeled as content versus form and then later modified as inner form versus outer form. The problem is that the distinction between the two aspects is difficult to maintain. After discussing this problem at some length they propose the following:

It would be better to rechristen all the aesthetically indifferent elements "materials" while the manner in which they acquire efficacy may be called "structure." This distinction is by no means a simple renaming of the old pair, content and form. It cuts right across the old boundary lines. "Materials" include elements formerly considered part of the content, and parts formerly considered formal. "Structure" is a concept including both content and form so far as they are organized for aesthetic purposes. The work of art is, then, considered as a whole system of signs, or structure of signs, serving a specific aesthetic purpose.[42]

A further elaboration of the same theoretical proposition appears in the following passage:

Instead of dichotomizing "form — content," we should think of matter and then of "form," that which aesthetically organizes its "matter." In a successful work of art, the materials are completely assimilated into the form: what was "world" has become "language." The "materials" of a literary work of art are, on one level, words, on another level, human behaviour experience, and on another, human ideas and attitudes. All of these, including language, exist outside the work of art, in other modes; but in a successful poem or novel they are pulled into polyphonic relations by the dynamics of aesthetic purpose.[43]

The theoretical approach advocated is that a work of literary art be seen in terms of the materials out of which it is created and the structure which holds these materials together and provides the aesthetic purpose which informs the whole work. The terms "materials" and "structure" could have been used in this study, but after considerable deliberation it was decided that since the object of the study was a novel, a term more appropriate than "structure" would be "world." The reason is that the unifying and aesthetic principle in the novel is many-sided and complex and more nearly approaches the concept of a world than that of a structure. Indeed Wellek and Warren do use the term "world" in reference to narrative fiction.

But the novelist offers less a case — a character or event — than a world. The great novelists all have such a world — recognizable as overlapping the empirical world but distinct in its self-coherent intelligibility. Sometimes it is a world which can be mapped out in some area of the globe — like Trollope's counties and cathedral town, Hardy's Wessex; but sometimes — as with Poe — it is not. Poe's horrendous castles are not in Germany or Virginia but in the soul.[44]

In my choice and use of the term "world" I am especially indebted to Professor James J. Y. Liu, who has so effectively used the term in his study of Chinese poetry. Professor Liu sees poetry as an exploration of worlds and of language.[45] But in approaching the *Hsi-yu pu* I do not see its world as projected by its language alone but by all of the materials, in themselves aesthetically indifferent, which Tung Yüeh has brought into his work. Thus, language is but one of three kinds of materials treated. These are much like the building blocks used by a mason, for they are similarly used by the author to produce his artistic creation. The world is both that which is projected by these materials and that which holds them together. Hence, it is through the world that the author finally realizes his artistic purpose.

In the critical study of Chapters 4 through 9 a conscious attempt has been made to apply the tools developed by Western literary criticism to an understanding of a late Ming Chinese novel. This is so not only with the basic theoretical approach taken from Wellek and Warren but also at various other points in the development of the study. Terms such as fable, satire, and myth, which come out of the tradition of Western literature, are applied to Chinese materials. I do not feel that any apologies are needed for doing this. The assumption implicit in such a practice is that there are universal principles which apply to all literature and if certain nomenclature refers to these principles which are apparent, as in the present case, in the literatures of both China and the West, then their use is justified even across the cultural barrier. Indeed, if the values of Chinese literature are to be communicated at all in English, and my study by its very nature attempts to do this, then certain universals are assumed in the exercise of transference of meaning through language. Having said this, however, I would add that great care must be maintained in the application of Western concepts and literary tools. This is especially true in the area of evaluation. The danger lies not so much in analyzing Chinese works for what they are in themselves with Western tools, but rather in trying to determine what they should or should not be in the light of improper comparisons with works from a different tradition. I have attempted to do the former but have rigorously eschewed the latter.

CHAPTER 2

# Tung Yüeh's Life and Works

## I Tung Yüeh's Ancestry

R ELYING on the *Nan-hsün chih,* a gazetteer on Nan-hsün Township compiled in 1922 by Chou Ch'ing-yün, Liu Fu has been able to trace Tung Yüeh's ancestry back fourteen generations.[1] At the beginning of this long line is Tung Chen-yüan, who during the Northern Sung reign of Cheng-he (1111–1118) emigrated from Hai-chou, which was located northeast of modern Tung-hai County (Tung-hai Hsien), Kiangsu Province. Tung Chen-yüan settled in Mei-lin Village (Mei-lin Li), now a part of Wu-hsing County, Chekiang Province.[2]

.Six generations later we come to the end of the Yüan dynasty and to Tung Cheng-szu, who together with his son Tung Jen-shou refused government service under the alien Yüan authorities. After the establishment of the Ming dynasty (1368), Tung Jen-shou was three times asked to serve under the new government but each time refused. It is said that he chiseled out a stone ship and retired in it.[3]

Tung Jen-shou had a grandson named Tung Hsiang, of whom we are told the following: "He tilled [his fields] and read [his books] but did not set foot in a city. He built a ten-foot room and in it hummed and sang. Above the door it read, 'Shih-hsi Chai' (Studio of Constant Practice) and by this he also styled himself."[4]

Tung Hsiang had a son named Tung Huan, who was a *sui-kung* (tribute student) during the Cheng-te reign period (1506–1522). Tung Huan lived until the age of sixty-three.[5]

Tung Huan had a son named Tung Pin, who in 1541 earned his *chin-shih* degree, ranking fifth on the list of successful candidates for that year.[6] Later Tung Pin served as *Li-pu tso-shih-lang* (Left Vice Minister of Personnel) and also as *Kung-pu shang-shu* (Minister of Works). He died in 1594 at the age of eighty-five.[7]

Tung Pin had a son named Tung Tao-ch'un, who earned his *chin-shih* in 1583. At that time Tao-ch'un was already fifty-one years old,[8] and then went on to serve as *Nan-ching kung-k'e chi-shih-chung* (Supervising Secretary in the Office of Scrutiny for Works in the Southern Capital).[9]

Tung Tao-ch'un had six sons. The eldest was Tung Szu-ch'eng (1560–1595),[10] who received his *chin-shih* in 1580, ranking fourth in his class,[11] and who later served as *Li-pu chu-k'e yüan-wai-lang* (Vice Director in the Bureau of Reception in the Ministry of Rites).[12] Tao-ch'un's third son, Tung Szu-chao, was also successful in the examinations, receiving his *chin-shih* in 1595.[13] Tao-ch'un's sixth and youngest son was Tung Szu-chang, Tung Yüeh's father.

We know that like his great-grandfather Tung Szu-chang was also a "tribute student" in the National University, but unlike his two elder brothers, mentioned above, he did not succeed in earning the *chin-shih* degree. Hsü Fu-ming suggests that the reason for this is that by his time the family had lost its influence politically.[14] His biographer in the *Nan-hsün chih* gives the following interesting information about him:

> He was wasted and thin and prone to illness. Acting independently and keeping to himself, he called himself the "thin recluse." As for earning a livelihood he was most clumsy and all he cared about were books. He copied by hand no less than one hundred portfolios. He read widely in the hundred philosophers and had a broad understanding of Buddhism and Taoism. In his life he had close friends who were all famous men of the world . . . and daily he would meet with them to deliberate over written works. Moreover he sincerely enjoyed discussing poetry. . . . [With his friends] he formed groups for successive recitation and strongly supported the teaching of poetry. He paid close attention to the historical records of Wu-hsing County, working both on supplements to bibliographies and also on monographs. Even when lying on his bed coughing up blood he still diligently worked with his writing brush. He died at the age of forty-two in 1628.[15]

There is some problem surrounding the date of Tung Szu-chang's death. The quotation above from the local gazetteer gives 1628, yet Tung Yüeh himself once wrote, "In the eighth year of my life I was called an orphan."[16] If Tung was born as we believe in 1620, then he is telling us here that his father died in 1627, which is one year earlier than that given in the gazetteer. Liu Fu accepts Tung's statement as the more reliable, suggesting that the *Nan-*

*hsün chih* needs correction at this point.[17] I am inclined to agree with Liu in this. Hsü Fu-ming, who has also addressed himself to this problem,[18] rejects Liu's conclusion as unwarranted, suggesting that Tung was born to his father's concubine and that when Tung said he was called an orphan his reference was to his being so called upon this woman's death. I find this theory hard to accept. Not only is it without solid evidence and seemingly based on Hsü's own speculation, but it also requires that Tung Yüeh be called an orphan (*ku-erh*) prior to his own father's death. It seems highly unlikely that this could happen, since in China when one's father died one was called *ku,* but when one's mother died one was called *ai.*

In reviewing Tung's ancestry, a number of points of significance may be brought out. First of all, it is clear that he came from a line of literary men. The *Nan-hsün chih* records one work by Tung Huan, four works by Tung Pin, three works by Tung Tao-ch'un, and fourteen works by Tung Szu-chang.[19]

Also we may note that in the three generations above Tung Yüeh the family had reached its peak in prosperity and worldly success. Two of Tung's uncles, his grandfather, and his great-grandfather all earned the coveted *chin-shih* degree. Both the great-grandfather and the eldest uncle ranked high on their respective lists of successful candidates. Perhaps the success of the family is best shown by the government posts held by the great-grandfather, grandfather, and eldest uncle, all three of whom are mentioned, though only briefly, in the official Ming history.[20]

Although success and prosperity had been experienced by the family, it is clear that by the time of Tung Yüeh's birth the family position was in rapid decline. Tung's father, although a "tribute student," did not succeed in the examinations and consequently was denied access to fame by way of the civil service. He was twenty-six years younger than his famous brother Tung Szu-ch'eng and must have found it hard to accept the fact that by the time he reached maturity the family's prospects had dimmed so considerably.

There is a strong tradition of eremitism and eccentricity apparent in Tung's early ancestry. Both Tung Cheng-szu and his son Tung Jen-shou declined government service. The latter clearly chose instead the life of a recluse. Tung Hsiang also takes his place in this tradition. When Tung Yüeh retired from the world, and when he showed himself to be somewhat eccentric, he was merely claiming his own place in this tradition.

## II   *A Sketch of Tung Yüeh's Life*

Tung Yüeh, whose courtesy name *(tzu)* was Jo-yü, was born in 1620 and died in 1686 at the age of sixty-six. Although his dates are not given in any of the early sources, they have been convincingly established by Liu Fu on the basis of the following three pieces of evidence.

First, there is a passage quoted from the *Lien-hua-chi sui-pi (Random Jottings from Chinaberry Jetty)* in which Tung Yüeh remembers how in the year *kuei-yu,* when he was thirteen years old, it was very dry and there were no continuous rains.[21] *Kuei-yu* was the sixth year of Ch'ung-chen, or 1633, which means that Tung Yüeh was born in 1620.

Further evidence is provided in a passage by Yü Yüeh (1821– 1906).[22] In his *Ch'un-tsai T'ang sui-pi (Random Jottings from Ch'- un-tsai Hall)* Yü says, "In examining Wang Hsieh-ch'eng's *Nan- hsün chih* we find that Tung Jo-yü died in the twenty-fifth year of K'ang-hsi, [the year] *ping-yin.* He was in his sixty-seventh year."[23] That is to say, Tung Yüeh died in 1686 at the age of sixty-six.

A final piece of evidence, this time only on the date of Tung Yüeh's death, is a quotation from Chang Chien (1768–1850) in which Chang tells how he was shown an old poem. The author of the poem had written, "On the sixth day of the fifth month of the year *ping-yin* Monk Pao-yün died, and on the thirteenth day I went and wept beneath [his] shrine."[24] Pao-yün is one of the Buddhist names used by Tung Yüeh, and the date given is equivalent to June 26, 1686.

We may assume that Tung Yüeh was both born and raised in his native place of Nan-hsün Township. Located seventy-two *li* east of the prefectural seat of Hu-chou, it bordered on Chen-tse County (Chen-tse Hsien) in Kiangsu. Until the reign of Kao-tsung of the Southern Sung (1127–1163) it was called Hsün-hsi, and later it was called Nan-lin. Then it was set up as a township *(chen)*, and finally during Tu-tsung's reign of the Southern Sung (1265–1275) it took on the present name of Nan-hsün. At the end of the Yüan dynasty the notorious Chang Shih-ch'eng, who had imperial aspirations, built a walled city at this place.[25]

Tung seems to have been very gifted as a child. A Ch'ing writer who called himself Chih-chiang Pao-yang-sheng (Pao-yang-sheng of Chekiang) tells how at the age of two Tung could sit cross-legged in Buddhist meditation, and at the age of four could read. Once in the presence of guests, when asked what book he wanted to read first, he said, "I want to read the *Yüan-chüeh ching (Sutra of Perfect Awareness)."* All who heard were amazed at him. After studying the sutra he then went on to the Four Books and the Five Classics.[26]

Three things stand out in Tung's early life as especially significant. The first is the strong Buddhist influence he experienced through his family. He tells us that when he was five and six years old, every year at the beginning of spring and on the Double Ninth his father saw to it that they all visited the various temples by the canal which ran past the town.[27] When Tung was seven years old he was copying Sanskrit and was being taught the *Hsin ching (Heart Sutra)*. Also, he tells us that at this early age he became a follower of Wen-ku Ta-shih (Grand Master Wen-ku), who gave him the Buddhist name of Chih-ling (Age of Wisdom).[28]

Tung also received the traditional Confucian training in the classics from an old friend of his father's named Chao Ch'ang-wen, and among his earliest recollections are those of experiences involving this tutor. In a selection in the *Ch'ien-chi* he writes:

At first when I was a boy I learned the books of Tsou and Lu from my tutor.[29] My tutor was sallow of complexion. His ancient garments would flutter in the wind and the Nan Shan cap [on his head] would shake. Although a boy, I knew in my mind that my tutor was not an ordinary man. For thirty years he had been friends with my father through poetry. When it came time for me to take instruction from my tutor, every evening my father would sit down and tell me to recite again the books I had read during the day. Before I had finished more than one or two lines, my father would suddenly cover the book and call out, "Young lad, stop. You must not tire yourself." In the morning he would then talk to my tutor and I felt pleased.[30]

In addition to the Buddhist influence and the influence of a classical tutor, we also see the strong influence of Tung's father. The quotation above shows that his father was actively involved in his early education, and Tung remembers his father as one who was lenient with him. This concern of the father for the welfare of his son is further revealed by the following passage, taken from the same selection quoted above:

When I was a young boy by nature I was not like other boys. I simply did not like to get up late. When the stars still glittered I would comb my hair and bathe. My father became greatly worried about this [and said], "Son, [if you act] like this you will become exhausted." He then instructed my tutor to order me to get up late. However, after a long time, there was no change. So he instructed my tutor to be harsh with me and order me to get up late. But my tutor could not bear to be harsh with me.[31]

Unfortunately his father died when Tung was only seven years old; yet the father's influence on his young son's later development must not be underestimated.

We may regard the death of Tung's father as marking the end of the early period of his life. The second period extends from this time on until Tung's first burning of his books in 1643, which was just one year before the official dynastic change.

During this period, which spans his life between the ages of seven and twenty-three, Tung continued his studies, now however giving particular attention to classical prose and especially to mastery of the examination style essay. Pao-yang-sheng tells us that at the age of nine Tung could write essays, at the age of twelve he entered the district school, and at the age of fifteen he became a salaried licentiate.[32] Tung must surely have entertained the hope shared by all well-educated and bright young men of his day that later he might succeed in the higher-level examinations and thereby gain an opportunity to launch into a civil-service career. Success in this would not only restore good fortune to Tung's family, but it would also provide a means for him to achieve fame through his ample literary talents. We know that for some time Tung studied under Hsü Ch'ih,[33] an official serving with the censoriate in his native province of Chekiang. Hsü Fu-ming tells us, moreover, that in 1639 Tung, together with a certain Yen Yu-ku and others, sat for a government examination. They all failed, however, because, as Hsü tells us, they could not provide the necessary money to bribe the examiners.[34]

During his late teens and early twenties Tung Yüeh wrote a great deal. He wrote the *Hsi-yu pu* around 1640 and his well-known *Ch'i-kuo k'ao* around 1641 or 1642.

It seems that after his father died Tung was left alone with his mother and was raised to maturity by her.[35] He once stated that he had no brothers,[36] and in his writings there seems to be no mention of sisters. We do not know anything at all about his wife nor do we know when he married.

During this time Tung became involved with the Fu She (Revival Society), but there is some dispute over the extent of this involvement. What is clear, however, is that for some time Tung was a student of Chang P'u (1602–1641), founder of the society. Soon after Chang's death Tung wrote three prose pieces. One is a prayer to his former teacher written on his own behalf,[37] and the other two, one a prayer to the deceased and the other a spiritual memorial for the deceased, were written "on behalf of fellow society members" (*tai t'ung-she*).[38] The Fu She was a politically oriented literary society, and from the identification in the latter two pieces we can see that Tung was surely involved with it.

The winter of 1643–1644 marks the beginning of a third period in Tung's life, for it is at this time that he carried out the first deliberate burning of his own works. This was later followed by two more burnings, the second taking place in the autumn of 1646 and the third in August 1656.[39] Tung tells us that in the first instance he destroyed all prose pieces he had written before he was twenty years old. The second burning included all essays in the examination style written during an earlier period covering more than ten years,[40] together with some miscellaneous works and poetry. The third burning was by far the most extensive. Tung reports that several hundred *chüan* of works were destroyed. If we are to take him at his word, he would have burned even more than this had not his son and others intervened and prevailed upon him to save some works for posterity.

Here an extremely important question presses in upon us. Why did Tung repeatedly burn his books? Liu Fu has suggested three possible reasons.[41] In going over his earlier writings Tung may have been dissatisfied with some which he now regarded to be of inferior quality, and so he chose to destroy them. In other words, the burnings may have been part of a general editing of earlier works done in connection with the compilation of various collections of his writings. A second possible reason is that after the beginning of the new dynasty Tung gave up all hope of pursuing an official career and so he destroyed all examination style essays which he had written with this hope still in mind. A third possible reason is that many of his works may have contained anti-Ch'ing sentiments. With the change of dynasty, these were now a source of great potential danger to him and so he carefully destroyed them. It seems reasonable to assume that all three of these factors played a part in the burnings. The extent to which emphasis is placed on one or another of these possible causes reflects in large measure one's broader understanding of Tung's life.

This period may be characterized as one of great change for Tung Yüeh. Like everyone else, he too was caught up in the vast political and social upheavals of the time. We know that he now became increasingly interested in Buddhism and in the life of seclusion. His biography in the *Nan-hsün chih* tells how, after the change of dynasty, he dismissed his students and shut himself up in his studio, which he called "Feng-ts'ao An" (Abundant Grass Hermitage), so that even his fellow-clansmen and relations did not see his face.[42] Pao-yang-sheng tells us that at this time he used his inherited wealth to provide for families that were hungry and cold.[43]

We also know that in 1645 he took his family and moved to Deer Mountain (Lu Shan).[44] He tells us that they traveled by boat.[45] In his writings there are other references to Deer Mountain,[46] and it may be that he and his family lived there for several years. The move was probably caused by the disruption which took place around this time accompanying the occupation of this southern area by the Ch'ing authorities.

In 1651 Monk Nan-yüeh was arrested by the new government.[47] Nan-yüeh was a leader of Ch'an Buddhism who made his headquarters at the famous Ling-yen Monastery, not far from modern Soochow,[48] and he had attracted a sizable following composed in part of Ming loyalists. After his arrest it seems that there was great confusion at the monastery, for his followers fled in all directions. Liu Ch'eng-kan, among others, tells us that Tung Yüeh, hearing of what had happened, immediately went up to the monastery and restored order.[49] For this courageous action Tung was highly respected by the leading men of the area.

In 1652 Tung wrote a piece in which he tells us how he changed his surname from Tung to Lin.[50] The next year he began to wear straw sandals and thus gave the first sure signs of a serious intention to become a monk.[51] We know that between 1653 and 1656 Tung made frequent trips to Mount Ling-yen.

Then on August 27, 1656, Tung took an oath never to write again.[52] He had now decided to make a complete break with his own past and with the human world. On August 29 he engaged in his third and final burning of books, then had his head shaved, took a Buddhist name, and became a monk at Ling-yen Monastery.

The fourth and last period of Tung's life extends from this time until his death thirty years later in 1686, and is characterized by a clearly discernible new-found freedom. This is revealed in two ways. First, Tung traveled around far more than he ever had before. For example, in 1666 he accompanied his spiritual teacher on a long trip to Hunan Province,[53] where he sailed on the Hsiang River, visited Heng-yang and Yüeh-yang, and spent some time in Changsha.[54]

Also, this freedom is revealed in the nature of his writings during this period. He did not, in fact, keep the vow he had taken never to write again. One suspects that the vow was more symbolic in nature than a declaration of true intent. In any case, Tung continued to write. He had been a prolific writer all his life and continued to be one after taking Buddhist vows. He now wrote an especially large amount of poetry, much of which is strongly Buddhist in outlook. His religious commitment provided for him an inner peace and serenity and a freedom from the cares of the world, all of which is revealed in his later writings.

During this period Tung held certain responsible positions in the Buddhist establishment. For some time he was in charge of the old Precious Cloud Ch'an Monastery (Pao-yün Ch'an-yüan) on Mount Yao-feng (Yao-feng Shan).[55] However, he does not seem to have stayed long in one location; instead, he traveled about a great deal, especially in the mountains. He was particularly fond of visiting remote and secluded places of outstanding scenic beauty, and on these travels he invariably took books along with him. Not long after his death Niu Hsiu wrote:

Everytime he [Tung Yüeh] went out traveling, fifty books were carried on a pole by someone following him. Despite the depth of remote valleys and the danger of vast billows he would not even temporarily be separated [from his books].[56]

Later tradition also tells how at this time he deliberately avoided social contacts. On one occasion, when two officials came to see him unannounced, he asked them to wait, saying that he needed to go to the toilet. This was a mere pretext, however, for he thereupon slipped out the side gate and fled across the lake.[57]

We are fortunate to have extant part of a diary Tung kept during this time. He was now living at a place he himself called Eastern Rocky Torrent (Tung-shih Chien).[58] The diary is the *Nan-ch'ien jih-chi (Diary of Nan-ch'ien),*[59] and covers the period of January 15 through July 21, 1676. It contains a total of 190 entries, one for each day with only one day missing (February 26).[60] The entries all follow a consistent pattern. The date is given by year, month, and day, the cyclical designation being used for both year and day. Then, usually, the weather is given. In some entries this is followed by a heading showing the topic of what is to follow. Some entries are long, running on for more than one hundred characters; others are short, with some giving only the weather. Entries contain such things as poetry, descriptions of visits from friends, descriptions of trips to other places, references to dreams, and general comments on all sorts of mundane experiences.

The significance of the diary lies not so much in the vast amount of factual information it contains (for much is trivial) as in the unique opportunity it affords for insight into the personality of Tung Yüeh, the man. He was a keen observer of nature and delighted in its changes. The diary takes us through winter, spring, and summer and shows that Tung identified himself with his environment and strove to live in harmony with it. The diary also shows that Tung had a great many intimate friends. These included his disciples, the names of several of whom occur repeatedly. Friends also frequently came to visit with him and to discuss questions of philosophy, religion, and art. The diary also reveals that Tung maintained correspondence with at least one of his sons. Tung obviously cared about these people and was open in his relationships with them. When one disciple became ill for a prolonged period, he recorded the details of this illness and his own efforts at a cure. The picture projected by the diary is that of a man who was happy, who maintained a positive attitude toward himself and his environment, who was content in his work, and who was well-adjusted in his relationships with friends and colleagues.

The biography in the *Nan-hsün chih* provides us with the last two important dates for this final period.[61] Tung's mother died in 1684,[62] and we are told that after her burial Tung returned to the mountains, never again to visit his native place. Tung himself died on June 26, 1686, at Evening Fragrance Monastery (Hsi-hsiang An).[63]

Tung had six sons, whose names were Ch'iao, Mu, Lei, Fang, Yü, and Ts'un. Ch'iao was born in 1639, Lei in 1642, and Ts'un in 1653.[64] We do not know when the other three were born. Ts'un died early, but we are told that the others all became well known, especially Ch'iao and Lei, who distinguished themselves as local poets.[65] Tung's collected works contain frequent references to his sons and it seems that he maintained a warm and intimate relationship with them throughout his life. We are told that when he became a monk his sons were all called his disciples.[66]

It is of interest to note that Chang Chien was one of Tung's descendants. Chang tells us that Tung was the father of his great-grandmother, and that from the time when Chang was eleven or twelve years old he remembers a certain Chin Ming-shih, who was Tung's great-grandson and also his own father's cousin. The line of descent is made even clearer when Chang also tells us that the retired scholar Tung Chia-yen was the nephew of his great-grandmother, and that this man lived in the Abundant Grass Hermitage of Nan-hsün, as did his father, Tung Shih-chi, his grandfather Tung Lei, and his great-grandfather Tung Yüeh.[67]

### III  *Tung Yüeh's Writings*

Although Tung burned a great many of his writings, nonetheless a large quantity still remains. These may be divided into two categories: those included in Tung's collected works, and those which have been handed down independently.

The collected works are known as the *Feng-ts'ao An chi* and have been reprinted in the *Wu-hsing ts'ung-shu,* which, as its name suggests, is a collectanea of works by men of Wu-hsing County, Chekiang Province. Liu Ch'eng-kan, the compiler and editor, was himself a man of Wu-hsing, and he has written a preface to the entire collectanea dated 1929.[68] However, the *Feng-ts'ao An chi* collection was brought together somewhat earlier than 1929, for Liu has included a postface to it dated mid-winter 1921–1922 (*hsin-yu chung-tung*). To a wood-block edition dated 1690, in twenty-five *chüan* (chapters), he added a *Hou-chi* in two *chüan* from a hand-written copy by the author. Thus, the present collection is in twenty-seven *chüan,* which are reprinted in eight *ts'e* (volumes).

It is divided into five parts. First, there is the *Feng-ts'ao An shih-chi,* a collection of poetry in eleven *chüan.* According to Tung's own preface, these poems were written between 1646 and 1656, and most likely the *Shih-chi* was put together not long before Tung burned his books the third time.

Second, there is the *Feng-ts'ao An ch'ien-chi,* or "former collection" of prose writings in six *chüan.* Probably this originally circulated as two collections, for Liu Fu describes a *Ch'ien-chi* which corresponds in content to only its first three *chüan,* and also a *Wen-*

*chi* which corresponds to its last three *chüan*.[69] Most likely Liu Ch'eng-kan combined the two into what he then simply called the *Ch'ien-chi*. The works in the first three *chüan* were written during the years 1640 to 1645 and those in the last three during 1646–1656. Thus, the last three *chüan* overlap those in the *Shih-chi* in time, and it is most likely, though never so stated by Tung, that these became a collection at the same time as did the *Shih-chi*.

Third, there is the *Feng-ts'ao An hou-chi,* or "later collection" of prose writings in two *chüan*. The works here are on religious and philosophical subjects, are highly polemic in nature, and many are written in the form of answers to questions. Only a few are dated, and those which are show that they were written late in Tung's life.[70]

Fourth, there is the *Pao-yün shih-chi* in seven *chüan,* which is another collection of poetry. In a preface to this by a nephew named Han-ts'e, dated the first lunar month of 1689, we are told that these poems were written after Tung became a monk, the last being written just one year before he died. As might be expected these show a strong inclination toward Ch'an Buddhism.

Finally, there is a collection called the *Ch'an yüeh-fu (Ch'an Ballads)* in one *chüan*. This contains forty-seven poems of what once was a longer collection. Many of the poems have rather extensive prefaces and notes and are thereby made the more interesting to the reader. They reflect Tung's study of the early *yüeh-fu* ballads which provided their inspiration.

Apart from the *Feng-ts'ao An chi,* there are six more works by Tung known to be extant today. These are, first, his novel the *Hsi-yu pu*. Second, there is the *Ch'i-kuo k'ao,* an historical work completed around 1641–1642 on the seven states of the Warring States period.[71] This work has been reprinted in numerous editions.[72] Third, there is the *Fei-yen-hsiang fa* in one *chüan*.[73] This is what we may call a pseudoscientific work in which Tung presents his method of producing smokeless, steamed incense. Part of it at least was completed in 1651.[74] Fourth, there is the *Nan-ch'ien jih-chi,* the diary of 1676 mentioned above.[75] Finally, there are two more works, neither of which I have seen: the *Lien-hua-chi sui-pi,*[76] and the *Feng-ts'ao An tsa-chu wu-chung*.[77]

Above I have given in cursory fashion known extant works by Tung Yüeh. These represent only a part of Tung's total literary output. Liu Fu gives a list of Tung's writings which appear in the *Nan-hsün chih*, and if the novel is added the total amounts to 112 works.[78] However, as Liu Fu points out, there are many problems with this list and probably Tung in fact wrote far less than this.[79] A number of important works by Tung were circulating a century after his death but are no longer extant today. The *Szu-k'u ch'üan-shu tsung-mu* includes five of Tung's works but only one of these, the *Ch'i-kuo k'ao,* has survived.[80] In this connection, it is interesting to note that the collected works survived in spite of the Ch'ien-lung literary inquisition; indeed a *Feng-ts'ao An chi* was included on one of the lists of prohibited books.[81]

Several scholars have paid special attention to Tung's works, and particularly to his poetry. Excluding now a consideration of his novel, the following may be given as examples. Chu Yi-tsun (1629–1709) included twelve of Tung's poems in his anthology, *Ming shih-tsung,* and suggested that Tung's "hard words and obscure style" (*ying-yü se-t'i*) distinguished him from others.[82] Hsü Tzu (1810–1862) included a short biography of Tung in his *Hsiao-tien chi-chuan pu-yi,* a book of biographies of eminent people of the Southern Ming. Hsü stated that Tung had over thirty collections of works (he listed seventeen of them) and that his poetry was "clear and light, wild and distant" (*ch'ing-tan huang-yüan*).[83] The late Ch'ing scholar Ch'en T'ien included thirteen of Tung's poems in his *Ming-shih chi-shih,* a work on Ming poets, and noted that Tung took refuge in Buddhism, used elegant phrases, and by his own description of himself was not like other poets.[84]

There is only one scholar, however, who has attempted a comprehensive evaluation of Tung's works and this is Liu Fu. Liu divides these works into the following nine categories: textual studies (*k'ao-chü shu*), anthologies (*hsüan-wen*), chronologies (*pien-nien shu*), scholarly studies (*yen-chiu hsüeh-wen-te chieh-kuo*), collections of poetry and prose (*shih wen chi*), fiction (*hsiao-shuo*), records of miscellany (*tsa-chi*), quotations (*yü-lu*), and books of miscellany (*tsa-shu*). He then analyzes the works on the basis of subject material and says that they fall under the following seven topical classifications: astrology and the study of signs (*t'ien-wen-tzu chi hsiang-shu-hsüeh*), history and chronology (*shih-hsüeh chi nien-li-hsüeh*), medicine (*yi-hsüeh*), etymology and phonology (*wen-tzu yin-yün-hsüeh*), versification and prosody (*yin-lü-hsüeh chi shih-ke-hsüeh*), Buddhism and Confucian-Buddhist eclecticism (*Fo-hsüeh chi Ju Fo he-ts'an*), and miscellaneous reading (*tsa-lan*).[85] Presumably the first classification is generically oriented and the second topically oriented, although this is never so stated. What emerges from Liu Fu's study is the realization that Tung's interests ranged widely and that Tung was a remarkably prolific and versatile writer.

CHAPTER 3

# Tung Yüeh's Personality and Activities

L IU Fu, the only modern Chinese scholar who has studied Tung Yüeh's life extensively, calls attention to Tung's natural literary talents and diligence in scholarly activities. Although he does not agree with Tung's eclectic approach philosophically and dismisses Tung's Ch'anist works as incomprehensible, Liu willingly accepts Tung's scholarly works as being quite good. Liu believes that if Tung had only concentrated on solid research he could have taken a place among the first-class scholars of China. The trouble as Liu sees it is that Tung did not do this but let petty and inconsequential matters lead him astray. When we come to Liu's understanding of the reason for this we are at the crucial point of Liu's whole evaluation of Tung Yüeh. Liu believes that all his life Tung suffered from a case of mental illness, and that it was this which in the end led Tung to be no more than a "second rate scholar half in a dream and half awake."[1]

## I *The Charge of Mental Illness*

Liu Fu believes that Tung inherited a tendency toward mental illness, and says:

From this we can see that [Tung Yüeh's father] Chieh-an was a very solitary and resolute man, a man with an exalted view of himself. Jo-yü in his veins also inherited this kind of disposition. However, Jo-yü's research and scholarship were broader than his father's in scope and greater than his father's in vigor. Therefore, in comparing the two, Chieh-an's temperament was inclined toward temerity, whereas Jo-yü's temperament was inclined toward madness. This is the point of difference between father and son.[2]

Liu then proceeds throughout his study to bring forward whatever evidence he can find to support this conclusion. Tung's state-

41

ment concerning his own childhood, in which he tells how as a very
young boy he had the habit of rising before dawn, is quoted by Liu
with this comment:

From this portion of the record we can know that Jo-yü was not only an
extremely intelligent child but also an extremely strange child. People who
in their youth are extremely intelligent and extremely strange in later years
cannot avoid signs of some mental illness. Therefore, later on, Jo-yü's
activities in life, his literary manifestations, and the road he took in
scholarship all clearly spring from a sick condition and not from health.
Fortunately in China there was still the way of "escape into Ch'an" which
could be taken, otherwise Jo-yü would probably not have been able to
avoid the tragic outcome of insanity or suicide which a great many western
writers have experienced.[3]

Citing Tung's habit of rising early as evidence of an inclination
toward mental illness, Liu argues that Tung displayed this inclination all his life, that this affected all his activities, writings, and
scholarship, and that his turn to Buddhism is to be explained primarily for its therapeutic value.

Liu contends that Tung's pseudoscientific works are nothing
more than the nonsense produced by a sick mind. Passages from
the *Fei-yen-hsiang fa (Method for Smokeless Incense)* are quoted to
substantiate this belief. Liu does recognize, however, that this is
nonsense "when seen from the viewpoint of a modern scientist."[4]
Furthermore, Tung's attitude toward his own writings is viewed as
an indication of mental and emotional instability. We are told that
Tung first reached a height of enthusiasm over a projected work
and either wrote it or started to write it, then felt depressed over it
and regretted what he had done, then burned the work, then vowed
never to write again, and then finally began the sequence all over
again. The result, we are told, is that Tung himself was in such a
state of confusion that, if asked, he could not even have given an
accurate account of his own works.[5]

Finally, Liu quotes Tung as having said that from birth he liked
to live on boats and listen to the rain,[6] and he adds three more
preferences to the list. We are told that he had a propensity for
dreams, and we are left in no doubt as to Liu's judgment on this.

One who is a monk ought to be at a great distance from confusion and
dreams, yet he [Tung] was a lofty monk who was exceedingly prone to
confusion and dreams.[7]

He is also said to have had the desire to invent new things. For instance, he tells us that after his son Ts'un was born he hit upon a new idea. He prepared a drink of shredded plum blossoms and milk and fed this to the infant.[8] Liu comments:

As for his carrying on in this confused way, making it sound better we may call it the juvenile way of poets, but making it sound worse we may call it a case of great mental illness.[9]

Liu also cites Tung's penchant for giving special names to people and things. Throughout his life Tung himself used more than twenty different names.[10] He not only picked names for himself but also invented names for his friends, as well as for places and objects of special significance to him.

Liu Fu's material is of great interest, but questions must be raised as to his use of it. Do we, in fact, have evidence here to warrant the conclusion that Tung was mentally ill? Careful study shows that other interpretations are possible. Just because Tung, as a boy, liked to get up early does not mean that he was inclined toward madness. As for Tung's pseudoscientific works, in all fairness to him they must be judged in the context of seventeenth-century China; one cannot blame Tung for not being a twentieth-century man and then proceed to accuse him of mental illness because of this. As for Tung's attitude toward his works, there is a great danger here of oversimplification. One cannot understand Tung's attitude, nor indeed his life at all, without reference to the larger political scene. Why was Tung filled with so much regret and what was it that he regretted? Why did he really burn his books? It is inadequate merely to suggest emotional instability and mental illness as an answer to these questions. Furthermore, there is good evidence to suggest that Tung took his writings very seriously indeed. Note, for example, the care with which he compiled various portions of his collected works. Much of the confusion which Liu attributes to Tung may well have been introduced by later bibliographers. As for Tung's personal peculiarities, other interpretations are also possible. Just because he was interested in dreams does not mean that he was confused or detached from reality. Indeed, his concern with dreams may suggest a desire to probe into the nature of reality itself. Likewise his propensity for the invention of new things may suggest an active, inquisitive mind rather than mental illness.[11] As for his propensity for giving special names to things, it is enough to point out that it was common for a man to have many names in seventeenth-century China.[12]

Liu's evidence, therefore, does not adequately support his mental-illness theory. The basic problem here, however, is really that of defining mental illness. A cursory survey of reference works shows that usually what is defined is "mental health" rather than "mental illness," and even with this there are difficulties. The *Encyclopaedia Britannica* states that "mental health cannot be defined with precision, since it is closely related to the customs and requirements of society. Since customs vary and societies differ, there is a multiplicity of variable factors."[13] Mental illness, which presumably is defined as the condition in which mental health does not prevail, is thus partly socially defined, and standards for its definition will vary in time and from one society to another.

On the other hand, there is evidence to support the view that Tung was quite healthy, both mentally and emotionally, at least in the later years of his life. The most intimate of all his writings, his diary, shows him to be a happy, well-adjusted person with a great many close friends. His life-style did not fit the standard Confucian ideal of the scholar-bureaucrat, and within that context his writings, filled as they are with flights of imagination, dreams, and fantasy, may well be seen as eccentric but not the aberrations of a man suffering from mental illness.

## II  *Tung Yüeh's Political Involvement*

Tung was born in 1620, the year which marked the end of the reign of the Wan-li emperor. A son, known as Kuang-tsung, was then put on the throne but only survived one month. He was followed by Hsi-tsung, who reigned from 1620–1627 under the era-name of T'ien-ch'i. The last of the officially recognized Ming emperors was Hsi-tsung's brother Szu-tsung, who reigned under the era-name of Ch'ung-chen from 1627 until the fall of the dynasty in 1644. Thus, Tung lived the first twenty-four years of his life under the last two Ming emperors.

This was a time of rapid deterioration for the Chinese state. Hsi-tsung, who seemed equipped neither with the intelligence nor the desire to rule effectively, allowed control of the government to slip into the hands of the ruthless eunuch Wei Chung-hsien. A time of terror followed, with morale among officials sinking to one of the lowest levels in all of Chinese history.

When Szu-tsung came to power he dismissed Wei Chung-hsien and made strenuous efforts to unite the country. However, by then it was too late. The Manchus were advancing in the northeast. They called their dynasty Ch'ing in 1636, revealing their dynastic ambitions by choosing a name obviously parallel to that of the Ming. At the same time, the peasants of China, unable any longer to bear the burden of crushing taxes and corrupt and unscrupulous officials, increasingly turned to rebel leaders for hope. Between 1641 and 1644, two of these, Li Tzu-ch'eng and Chang Hsien-chung, seriously entertained dynastic ambitions themselves.[14]

The official collapse came in 1644 when the Manchus, who had occupied Peking, claimed succession to the Mandate of Heaven. There was a prolonged period of years stretching out before and after this date, when much of China was in turmoil with widespread suffering. The crisis was not confined to the North and West, where Li Tzu-ch'eng and Chang Hsien-chung carried on most of their activities, but was felt also in the rich lower–Yangtse River area where Tung lived.

At least twice in his life Tung was identified with politically active persons and groups. As has been stated, Chang P'u, the founder of the Fu She, was his teacher; when Chang died in 1641 Tung wrote three memorial pieces for his late teacher, one independently and two "on behalf of fellow society members." Also, in 1651 Tung went to Mt. Ling-yen and restored order at the monastery there after its leader, Monk Nan-yüeh, was arrested. Nan-yüeh was a staunch Ming loyalist and well known for his political activities.

Tradition tells us that Tung instructed his sons to "give up examination-style writings and to end their days in cotton and hides,"[15] and it seems that his sons followed these words and did not serve the Ch'ing authorities. Tung's exhortation was presumably given in his old age, which suggests that he remained a Ming loyalist to the end.

On this question of Tung's political involvement, Liu Fu and Hsü Fu-ming disagree. Liu doubts that Tung was politically active. He admits that Tung must have had some sort of relationship with the Fu She but takes as convincing the argument that Tung was too young to have played a significant role in the society.[16] As for the courageous trip to Mt. Ling-yen, Liu doubts that it was ever made. He reasons that none of Tung's writings for 1651 makes any reference to it or to anything connected with it.[17]

On the other hand, Hsü Fu-ming not only affirms Tung's active involvement with the Fu She and with the Buddhist loyalists but interprets the whole of Tung's life, including all of his activities and the motivations behind them, as inspired by a deep sense of political commitment and a fervent patriotism. Thus, Hsü contends that in his youth Tung observed the increasing corruption and moral degradation of the official class and the gradual weakening and final collapse of the state. In protest against this and with the desire to bring about reform he studied under Chang P'u and enrolled as a member of the Fu She.[18] Hsü believes that through his writings, and especially through his *Hsi-yu pu,* Tung expressed these deeply felt sentiments. He argues that when the Manchus founded the new dynasty, Tung, as a patriotic Chinese, remained loyal to the Ming, and so refused to serve the Manchus and instructed his sons not to do so as well. He was active in Ming loyalist activities all his life and for this reason became increasingly more involved with Monk Nan-yüeh. Hsü concludes that Tung's religious involvement was really just a "cover-up" for his loyalist activities.

Thus, Liu and Hsü hold very different views on the question of his political involvement. Liu writes: "With the exception of his writings, throughout his life Jo-yü did practically nothing at all."[19] And as for his writings, Liu sees these as unfortunately marred by second-rate material produced by a sick mind. Hsü, on the other hand, sees Tung as an arch-patriot, zealous for reform in his youth and in his later years unswerving in his loyalty to the native Ming dynasty.

Both of these views are somewhat extreme. It is impossible to deny that in his youth Tung was involved with the Fu She, which Liu seems reluctant to admit. Also, there is no reason whatever to doubt the veracity of the account of the trip to Mount Ling-yen in 1651.[20] Liu's argument that Tung's writings for that year contain no references to the trip carries little weight. Had Tung written anything about the trip he would surely have burned this along with the other writings in 1656 because of the clear danger to himself in not doing so. However, to carry the meaning and extent of Tung's political involvement as far as Hsü does is certainly not warranted. If it is wrong to suggest that Tung did nothing more than write, it is also wrong to suggest that he was a lifelong political activist.

### III   *Tung Yüeh and Buddhism*

There is one aspect of Tung's life which is passed over as only tangentially important by both Liu Fu and Hsü Fu-ming. This is Tung's involvement with Buddhism.

Liu dismisses Tung's Ch'anist writings as incomprehensible and regards his philosophical works as valueless, simply because "Confucianism, Buddhism, and Taoism fundamentally cannot be united."[21] However, in his adherence to Ch'an Buddhism and in his espousal of an eclectic philosophical approach Tung was very much a man of his times. His religious commitment was based on his understanding of the nature of man and reality, and in this he shared the company of many intellectuals.

As for Hsü's position, in which the political factor dominates, one may agree that there is a mixing of political and religious elements in his involvement with Monk Nan-yüeh, but to conclude that political considerations were paramount is wrong. Hsü tells us that Tung's decision to become a monk was:

...mainly inspired by a feeling of intense patriotism, for since he was unwilling to abandon the people's stand to become a slave of the new dynasty and was unable under the suppression of the Ch'ing dynastic regime to engage in open armed struggle, he could not but submerge himself in the Ch'an school and by proclaiming the way of the Buddha spread around patriotic thoughts.[22]

Hsü sees Tung's religious involvement primarily as a means toward achieving a political end and rejects the idea that Tung either found or even tried to find any final solution for life in Buddhism. Yen K'e-chün wrote a poem on a painting depicting Tung, and it contains these two lines about him:

> He must just sweep away his regret over the
>     rise and fall [of the empire],
> And [sitting] peacefully and serenely on his
>     reed mat enter into meditation.[23]

Liu Fu quotes these lines at the beginning of his study.[24] Hsü refers to this quotation to show how Liu and presumably Yen and others had misunderstood Tung's real intention in becoming a monk.[25] Hsü does not believe that Tung had any desire to "sweep away his regret," and he does not see Tung's Buddhist involvement as an attempt to do this.

Tung's collected works contain a large amount of material on Ch'an Buddhist themes which cannot have been written out of political motivation. Also Tung's diary shows him, at least in 1676, to have been a man living a serenely peaceful, religious life with no apparent interest in politics.

Liu and Hsü both fail to allow for an adequate complexity in Tung's life. Each has seized upon what indeed is a significant feature. For Liu it is Tung's eccentricity (or neurosis) and for Hsü it is his patriotism. Tung was, however, a complex human being and one for whom Buddhist beliefs were far from insignificant.

Neither Liu nor Hsü considered the importance of change in Tung's life. For Liu, once an eccentric always an eccentric, and for Hsü, once a patriotic loyalist always a patriotic loyalist. Continuities, no matter how real, should not block our view to significant changes in life-styles, and the fact is that Tung went through at least one great change when he gave up his family and home and became a wandering monk at the age of thirty-six.

The influence of Buddhism pervaded his life. He was born into a home in which Buddhism was practiced and in which Buddhist values and teachings were highly regarded. Some of his earliest recollections are of experiences involving temples and monks. At a tender age he began not only to study the Confucian classics but also various Buddhist scriptures and Sanskrit.

Buddhist ideals maintained their hold on Tung throughout his years as a young man. This includes the period when he was involved politically, as is demonstrated by the *Hsi-yu pu*. Written when Tung was only twenty, the novel is informed by a profound Buddhist view of the world, man, and reality in general.

When the change of dynasty came it was natural for Tung to gravitate toward loyalist Buddhist groups. At this time, however, a gradual change is perceptible. More experienced in life and matured in his thinking, Tung now decided to commit himself entirely to the Buddhist way, and after years of preparation he became a monk. It is not possible to know to what extent the decision was initially motivated politically. What is clear, however, is that by the end of his life he had immersed himself in Ch'anist doctrine and practice, had removed himself from secular society, and by all indications was at peace with himself and the world.

It is not insignificant that Tung chose to become a Ch'an Buddhist monk. Ch'an emphasized the intuitive method of spiritual training and Tung, with his highly sensitive personality and imaginative mind, was clearly attracted to it. Tung's spiritual master, Monk Nan-yüeh, was a leader in the Lin-chi school of Ch'an.[26]

This was one of the early Ch'an schools begun as far back as the T'ang dynasty, with Yi-hsüan as its recognized founder.[27] In Ming times it was one of the leading schools of Ch'an and differed from its chief rival, the Ts'ao-tung school, by the methods it used to achieve enlightenment. Kenneth S. Ch'en has described these methods as follows:

The Lin-chi branch ... follows what may be called the shock therapy, the purpose of which is to jolt the student out of his analytical and conceptual way of thinking and lead him back to his natural and spontaneous faculty. To achieve this the master shouts at his disciple or administers a physical beating to him. Or, in response to a question put by the student, he replies with an answer seemingly unrelated to the question.[28]

A thorough understanding of the influence of Buddhism on Tung's life will require more extensive study, but it is possible at this stage to see that Buddhism was an essential factor in his life.

## CHAPTER 4

# *Verbal Materials (Language) in* Hsi-yu pu

F OLLOWING Wellek and Warren's concept of literature as composed of materials which are united in structures, or to use the terminology I have adopted, worlds, we must first turn our attention to the materials in the novel. For the sake of convenience these are divided into verbal, narrative, and conceptual materials. The verbal materials are treated first, as they appear to be most fundamental. They can exist independently, whereas both the narrative and conceptual materials require the verbal for articulation.

What is aimed at in this chapter is not an exhaustive study but rather a general survey. My purpose is twofold: to show the kinds of verbal materials out of which Tung constructed his novel and where possible to explain the functions of these; second, to show how the verbal materials are used in particular ways to realize specific purposes and to create special effects.

## I *Use of the Vernacular*

The basic medium of expression in the novel is the vernacular language. Within the Chinese context this refers to a style of the written language which most nearly approximates colloquial speech and is to be contrasted with the classical language.[1] By Tung's time vernacular fiction had developed through a long tradition, and the tradition prescribed not only technique but also language.

The standard colloquial of China was and is that of the north, and specifically that of Peking, the capital.[2] However, colloquial speech in China is distinguished by broad dialect groups and there is considerable variation even within a single given dialect. The fact that the vernacular is used in the novel and that this takes northern Chinese as its pattern suggests a considerable accomplishment for Tung, who was a native of Chekiang Province. His own native speech was the southern Wu dialect, and to write in the standard vernacular meant to write in a medium based on a dialect considerably different from his own. Coming from a scholarly family, however, with uncles who served in high government positions, he was undoubtedly exposed from childhood to the *kuan-hua* (language of the officials), which was based on the language of the capital. This surely facilitated his mastery of the written vernacular.

For the most part Tung's vernacular fits the standard form, and as such it covers a range which includes several different levels. At one end there is the vulgar vernacular and at the other end the semi-literary vernacular. This range is invariably used to reveal and reinforce social rank and distance which do exist even in a novel of fantasy such as the *Hsi-yu pu.*

There are several indicators of level, and these include not only choice of vocabulary but also distinctive word order and syntax. One common indicator is the choice of pronouns. In familiar speech the characters in the novel invariably use the common colloquials *wo, ni,* and *t'a.* For instance, in the first dialogue in Chapter 1 the T'ang Monk speaks to Monkey and uses both *wo* and *ni.*[3] However, when the emperor appears as he does in Chapters 2 and 3, of course, he uses the imperial first-person pronoun *chen,*[4] and is addressed as *pi-hsia* (English equivalent, Your Majesty).[5] The greatest range of usage of pronouns is by Hsiang Yü, who in his speeches in Chapters 6 and 7 regularly uses for the first person the classical *wu,* the general colloquial *wo,* and the Shantung colloquial *an.*[6] The last is of some possible significance, for Hsiang Yü was a native of northern Kiangsu, which is not too far from Shantung. Perhaps a bit of subtle satire is intended here and this may lie in the irony that in spite of his status as a general, he still speaks vulgarly like an uneducated and uncouth Shantungese.

The vulgar level is also indicated by other highly colloquial expressions. The sweeping maid in Chapter 2 makes her appearance saying, "Ha, Ha, the emperor is asleep and the chief ministers are also asleep."[7] Other colloquial words include *ts'ui,* usually an exclamation indicating dissatisfaction or disgust;[8] *hai,* a general affirmative exclamation;[9] *ya,* either a final particle with an implication of suggestion or an interrogative particle used in the first half of a choice type question;[10] *ai yao,* an exclamation of alarm;[11] and *t'a t'a,* used adverbially as an indication of disappointment.[12] Also, the noun suffix *erh* is used frequently.

The level of language rises appropriately for a correspondingly higher level of social context. For instance, in Chapter 5 the dialogue among Monkey, who is in disguise as Beauty Yü (Yü Mei-jen), and the three lovely ladies is that of polite society and is filled with frequent classical forms and expressions. This is also true of the parts of Hsiang Yü's speeches where he adjusts his language to the situation. This sometimes leads to an interesting mixture of levels. For instance, at one point Hsiang Yü says, "Wu pien he-tao, 'Ni chiao shen-ma ming-tzu?' " (I then called out and asked, What is your name?).[13] Here the first part of the sentence, directed to Beauty Yü, is in the polite, semiclassical form whereas the quotation, directed at an unknown soldier, is in an extremely colloquial form.

The use of the vernacular creates certain effects and allows for certain functions characteristic of most Chinese vernacular fiction. Yet these similarities do obscure the fact that the novel is different in significant respects from much other vernacular fiction.

In contrasting vernacular prose with classical prose Hanan has shown that whereas the vernacular tends to be "referential and denotative," the classical tends to be "elegant and evocative," and whereas the vernacular tends to be "exhaustive," the classical tends to be "concentrated and elliptical."[14] Hanan goes on to state that although there is change evident through time, the validity of these distinctions holds.

Though the vernacular narrative prose does change — one finds in the Ch'ing dynasty novels a greater tendency to use the vernacular evocatively — the denotative-exhaustive use is still paramount, and may be regarded as the staple kind in vernacular fiction.[15]

For Hanan, this distinction marks the formal aspect necessary for genre identification. The corresponding nonformal aspect is the way in which reality is depicted through what Ian Watt has called "formal realism."[16] Here there is an interest in particularity understood both historically and spatially.

In the *Hsi-yu pu* the vernacular is both denotative and exhaustive. That is to say, the method of presentation is direct. There is much detailed description of actions, situations, and events.

Sequences of materials are presented with attention to order and transition. However, the adjectives "denotative" and "exhaustive" can only be applied in terms of the world of the *Hsi-yu pu* itself and not in terms of formal realism as described by Hanan. Later I shall show that this world is one of dream, satire, and myth. Manifestly this is not the same world as that of the formal realists. There is a realism in the novel at the level of dream analysis where Tung is clearly trying to show us how he believes dreams actually work. Yet this is not historical or spatial realism. Furthermore, in terms of the novel as a whole and its promotion through its theme of the Buddhist world-view, it is by its concern for highly abstract philosophical and religious ideas both evocative and elliptical. Thus, the vernacular here suggests that the novel fits only one-half of Hanan's formula. The language is denotative and exhaustive within the context of its own world. It does not, however, support a formal realism historically or spatially oriented but rather its own understanding of reality. The novel is thus at points similar to and at other points different from the kind of realistic vernacular fiction described by Hanan.

## II  *Classical Prose Passages*

In addition to the basic vernacular medium, Tung has also brought into his work a variety of other types of verbal materials, and these may conveniently be considered under the two general categories of classical prose passages and verse forms. It is possible to read the novel and to isolate the following classical prose materials:

1. Monkey's prayer to departed spirits.[17]
2. Quotations from official records.
    a. The passages read out by the emperor from the *Huang T'ang pao-hsün (Precious Teachings of the Imperial T'ang).*[18]
    b. The excerpts from the three court cases on Ch'in Kuei read and criticised by Monkey.[19]

This material is all, of course, purely fictitious and is presented in the interest of the narrative demands. In contrast, however, are the following:

    c. The series of passages taken from Ch'in Kuei's record and read to him at his trial.[20]

With the exception of the last section of this series which gives an account of Yüeh Fei's death, these are based upon material in Ch'in Kuei's biography in the official history of the Sung dynasty.[21]

3. An imperial mandate sent out from the New T'ang.[22]
4. An examination essay.[23]
5. A Taoist prayer of exorcism.[24]
6. Formal correspondence.
   a. The return letter from Lao-tzu to Monkey while Monkey serves as judge in hell.[25]
   b. The letter of the caretaker Shen to Wang the Fourth.[26]
7. The telling of Monkey's fortune.[27]
8. A bill of divorcement.[28]
9. Records of accounts.[29]
10. Military orders.[30]
11. Short passages.
    a. The inscription on the wall of the New T'ang.[31]
    b. The inscription above the Lü-yü Tien (Green Jade Hall) and on its walls.[32]
    c. The announcement of the three top successful candidates in the government examination.[33]
    d. The inscription on the stone plaque in the World of the Ancients.[34]
    e. The notice tacked on Nü Wa's gate.[35]
    f. The inscription on Hsiang Yü's banner.[36]
    g. The banner inscriptions and opening proclamation in the court of hell.[37]

With the exception of the record on Ch'in Kuei, these passages appear to have been composed independently by the author for the novel. They are used to fill a narrative need, to fill out the story by providing it with special types of verbal materials, to advance the narrative smoothly through its transitions, and in general to make the whole novel a great deal more interesting and enjoyable than it would be without them. The related function of providing humor will be taken up later. The passages in classical prose also serve an important artistic function. They demonstrate the author's literary skill. He not only shows his command of the vernacular, but he also demonstrates that he can employ equally well the various classical styles.

### III    *Verse Forms*

There are over fifty passages of verse incorporated into the novel's sixteen chapters, and these range in length from single matching lines of poetry and drinking games to a long ballad of 114 lines. These may be classified under the various forms they take.

1. Couplets.
   a. The sixteen seven-syllable chapter subheadings.[38]
   b. The seven-syllable couplet on those in sorrow in Chapter 5.[39]
   c. The seven-syllable couplet on the mind that is upright in Chapter 16.[40]
   d. The couplet on the door of the hexagram palace in Chapter 11, each half of which takes on the pattern 3–3–4.[41]
2. The four-syllable quatrain on a scroll in Chapter 12.[42]
3. Five-syllable quatrains.
   a. The quatrain in Chapter 2 given in support of the description of the New T'ang, and a note indicates that this is an old verse.[43]
   b. The quatrain seen by Monkey's fine hairs written on a wall in Chapter 11.[44]
   c. The quatrain heard by Monkey's fine hairs as sung by immortals in Chapter 11.[45]
4. Seven-syllable quatrains.
   a. The quatrain introducing the theme at the beginning of Chapter 1.[46] An original note indicates that this is an old verse.
   b. The quatrain recited immediately before the presentation of the ballad in Chapter 12.[47]
   c. The song sung by Ts'ui-sheng Niang (Maid Kingfisher Cord) in Chapter 14.[48]
   d. The quatrain describing the soldier in Chapter 15.[49]
5. The seven-syllable regulated verse given in reference to the beauty of the peonies in Chapter 1; an original note indicates that this is an old verse.[50]
6. *Gathas.*
   a. The *gatha* recited by the T'ang Monk in Chapter 1 on the redness which is in the disciple's heart (4–4/4–4).[51]
   b. The *gatha* Monkey recites for Yüeh Fei in Chapter 9 (4–4/4–4).[52]
   c. The *gatha* recited by the Hsü-k'ung Tsun-che (Venerable One of the Void) in Chapter 16 on the meaning of monkey's dream. It is given in forty-four paired five-syllable lines.[53]
7. Verses in uneven lines not specified as *gathas.*
   a. The description in Chapter 5 of the beauties on the Wo-hsiang T'ai (Grasping Incense Terrace) (3–3–3–3/5–5).[54]
   b. The song heard by the T'ang Monk and Prince Little Moon in Chapter 12, wafted to them by the wind (7–7–8–7/8–9–9–7).[55]
   c. The song of the fisherman in Chapter 13 (7–7/11–5–5–3–3).[56]
   d. The song of the Taoist and the five immortals given on stage in Chapter 13 (7–8/6–4–4).[57]

e. The description of the army prepared for battle in Chapter 15 (4–4/4–6–3–3–4/4–6–3–3–4/4–6–4–4–6/7–7).[58]

f. Pigsy's verse to the Monk turned general in Chapter 15 (3–3–7–7/7–7/3–7–7/7–7).[59]

g. Monkey's verse to the Monk turned general in Chapter 15 (5–5/7–7/7–10).[60]

8. The ballad.

This, the longest verse in the novel, is found in Chapter 12.[61] In Chinese, the form is called *t'an-tz'u*. *T'an* means to play a stringed instrument, and *tz'u* refers to the words of a song. The form is one in which verse was spoken or sung to musical accompaniment. It originally developed out of the practice of folk artists who recited and sang to stringed accompaniment material usually of a narrative nature.[62] It reached its height of popularity in the Ming, and by the end of the dynasty had attracted the attention of literary men who imitated it and used it as a new form for their own literary creations. Yeh Te-chün, in his study of chantefable literature in the Sung, Yüan, and Ming dynasties, refers to Tung's ballad and concludes that it did not have an independent existence apart from the novel.[63] He takes it to be Tung's own creation and believes that in writing it Tung was imitating a popular current folk-art form.

The ballad is entitled "Hsi-yu t'an" (The Ballad of the Westward Journey) and is presented as sung to the accompaniment of a lute. Consisting of 114 lines, mostly seven-syllables in length, it is given in two parts. After a musical introduction, there are fifty-four lines of verse.[64] After a prose interlude, fifty-six more lines follow. In content the ballad covers the story of the journey, beginning with creation and ending with Monkey's delay in the Myriad Mirror Tower.

9. Miscellaneous matching lines.

Included here are the various lines composed during the poetry and drinking games by Monkey and the three beauties on the Grasping Incense Terrace in Chapter 5.[65] The method followed is for one line to be given by the leader and matching lines to be supplied by the other participants with drinking penalties meted out for failure to comply. The lines are of varying lengths and their significance lies chiefly in the way they demonstrate the author's skill. He not only supplies the necessary matching lines, but he also reflects Monkey's personality in the lines he has Monkey compose.

The above survey will show the great variety of verse materials which Tung brought into his novel. It is unclear how many of these were his own creations and how many he borrowed or adapted from other sources. Notes in the original edition give three poems as "old poems." Two of these (3a and 5 above) serve a strictly decorative function, whereas the third (4a above) is important to the novel's theme. Most of the verse materials are closely integrated either into the narrative or conceptual framework and this would suggest that they were composed by the author himself.

Six verse passages are presented as sung. Four of these are in uneven lines. The patterns here suggest that established tunes were being followed. However, none of these have been identified as yet.

Frequently the verse materials serve the function of meeting narrative demands. This is clearly the case, for instance, with the verses used in the poetry games. In general, however, narrative demand is less important as a function for verse than for prose materials. The chief function of the verse materials is artistic. They raise the aesthetic quality of the novel and in doing so both demonstrate the literary skill of the author and make the novel more interesting and enjoyable for the reader.

## IV   *The Language and Imagery*

An examination of the verbal materials of the novel necessarily assumes not only consideration of the separate kinds and functions of language in the novel, but also consideration of special effects created by and specific purposes realized through the use of language.

The novel is rich in imagery. Both the story and the theme make the extensive use of imagery natural and necessary. One expects to find in dreams strange and unusual images, and the very fact that Tung Yüeh chose to write about a dream opened up the possibility for him of exercising to the utmost his powers of fantasy. Moreover, the dream is not that of a common mortal but of a superhuman monkey. Not only the story but also the Buddhist theme promotes the use of imagery. Religious expression is commonly characterized by symbolic language, and imagery associated with the Buddhist theme is natural and expected. The imagery is of various kinds. Some is referred to by literal description, some by allusion, and some by the devices of metaphor and simile.

However, in addition to the general use of imagery, Tung engages in a most interesting practice of providing us with passages composed entirely of long strings of images. There are three clear examples of this.[66] The first, translated below, is the list in Chapter 1 of twenty-five colors given as the colors of the robe the children will have made for themselves. The second is the list in Chapter 3 of the sixteen items sent with the imperial mandate recalling the T'ang Monk.[67] The third is the list in Chapter 4 of twenty-seven mirrors in the Wan-ching Lou (Tower of Myriad Mirrors).[68] These strings achieve a unique effect quite different from that created through the normal use of imagery. To examine this usage more closely, the passage in which the list of colors appears follows:

By nature the Elder was fond of quietness. How could he stand the children taunting him so? He tried to send them off with kind words, but they would not go. He reprimanded them, but still they would not go. They just shouted out, "This boy has grown up but is still wearing the hundred-family-garment."[69] There was nothing much the Elder could do but take off his cassock, put it away in his knapsack, and sit down on the grass. Those children didn't pay any attention to him. Again they shouted out, "Give us that one-colored hundred-family-garment of yours. If you don't give it to us we shall go home and ask our mothers to make a hundred-family-garment for us and it will be made up of

> the color of green duck-weed,
> the color of begonias,[70]
> the color of green willows,
> the color of one-winged conjugal birds,[71]
> the color of a glowing sunset,
> the color of swallow black,[72]
> the color of bean sauce,
> the color of Heaven's darkness,
> the red color of peaches,
> the color of jade,
> the color of lotus meat,
> the color of green lotuses,
> the color of silver seals tied with green ribbons,[73]
> the white color of fish stomachs,
> the color of liquid ink,
> the color of pale red and white mountain flowers,[74]
> the color of flowering rushes,[75]
> the color of green
> the five colors,[76]
> the color of brocade,
> the color of the lichee,
> the color of coral,
> the green color of a duck's head,
> the color of palindrome brocade,[77]
> the color of red berry brocade.[78]

And we won't want your one-colored hundred-family-garment. The Elder closed his eyes, remained in silence and did not answer.[79]

There are several things to note about this passage. The first is that both in length and content the list of colors fulfills functions other than those demanded by the narrative. The list is long, with twenty-five separate images, and although a robe of twenty-five colors is conceivable, close examination will show that in fact there are not twenty-five separate colors at all. Green, for instance, is followed by the five colors which include green. Images such as jade, brocade, and coral suggest several possible colors. This leads to the conclusion that the primary focus here is not on the colors themselves but on the imagery connected with them. The images are vivid and suggestive of all sorts of sensual pleasures, and in the chapter on conceptual materials, these images will be related to the theme of the novel, and it will be shown how this robe is contrasted with the one-colored robe of the Monk.[80]

In terms of its effect, this passage causes the mind of the reader to be shaken loose from the logic of common language and to focus directly on the imagery. In part then its function is to elicit a response which is directly prompted by the images themselves and not by the rational structure of the passage. We may well call this the intuitive approach and may possibly see here the influence of Tung's involvement with Ch'an Buddhism. In this, as well as in the other two lists mentioned above, the images seem to flow freely from Tung's unconscious mind. This outpouring resembles the results of the free associational techniques used in modern psychology, and constitutes one of the most striking uses of language in the novel.

## V    *The Language and Allegory*

One allegorical scheme is carried throughout the whole novel, and this is both created and supported by a particular use of language. Various words are used to stand for the Buddhist concept of desire. The key word here is *ch'ing,* which basically means "emotion." In the Buddhist context this refers to desire by which man becomes attached to the transient world and which is the cause of his suffering. By several clever devices, words representing objects as well as names of characters and places are associated with this concept.

The chief device used is that of the pun. Although the word for desire itself seldom occurs, two of its homonyms are used frequently. Thus, we have first the Ch'ing-yü Ching (Mackerel Spirit), and in the novel this fish spirit clearly stands for desire. When

Monkey is caught under the spell of the Mackerel, he is in fact caught by his own desire. The last line of the *gatha* recited by the Venerable One of the Void reads: And there was no Mackerel, for this was Monkey's desire.[81]

The other homonym is the word for green or green-blue, *ch'ing,* and this also supports the allegorical scheme by representing desire. The following are selected examples of its use:

1. When the T'ang Monk and his disciples first come upon the lush scene with the peonies, the women, and their children, the Monk is suspicious and expresses a fear that something calamitous may occur. He refers to the place as a *ch'ing-ch'ing ch'un-yeh* (green, green spring wilderness).[82]
2. During much of Monkey's dream he is in the Ch'ing-ch'ing Shih-chieh (Green, Green World) of Prince Little Moon.[83]
3. When the T'ang Monk is commissioned as a general he is called *Sha-ch'ing kua-yin ta-chiang-chün* (Great General Slayer of the Green).[84]
4. The mirror for the World of the Ancients is the Lou-ch'ing Ku-ching (Ancient Mirror Carved in Green).[85]
5. In the Green, Green World there is the Ch'a-ch'ing-t'ien Lou (Pavilion Protruding into the Green Sky).[86]
6. When the Mackerel appears in the disguise of a new disciple he is called Wu-ch'ing (Aware of Green).[87]

In addition to the direct pun, there is also the indirect device of using synonyms for green to stand for desire. Thus we have:

1. The *lü-chin ch'i* (green brocade flag) flying over the New T'ang.[88]
2. Lü-chu Nü-tzu (Lady Green Pearl) in the World of the Ancients.[89]
3. The *lü-shui* (green water) into which Monkey is pushed when he leaves the Wei-lai Shih-chieh (World of the Future).[90]
4. The *lü-tzu* (green characters) on the scroll in the Green, Green World.[91]
5. The Lü-chu Tung (Green Bamboo Cave) of the old Taoist fortuneteller in Chapter 13.[92]

Other examples could be given not only of the use of this synonym, *lü,* but also of various shades of green such as those found in the list of colors quoted above. In fact, the novel is filled with words suggesting greenness or shades of greenness.

A third device is that used in arriving at the name of Prince Little

Moon. What Tung has done here is to take the character *ch'ing* (emotion, desire) and break it down into three component parts, which produce characters resembling *hsiao* (little), *yüeh* (moon), and *wang,* (prince). Thus, the name of this central figure is written with three characters which when put together may graphically yield the character for desire.[93]

There is obviously a danger here of carrying this allegorical interpretation too far. The temptation to see more significance than is justified in various linguistic relationships must be guarded against. Indeed, many words have some relationship with each other either phonetically or graphically but the relationship may not be significant. Surely not every word either homophonous with desire or homophonous with any of its synonyms necessarily stands for desire. Nevertheless, regardless of how far one chooses to carry the scheme of the allegory, it is clear that there is such a scheme and that it represents an important use of language.[94]

## VI   *The Language and Humor*

From beginning to end the novel is informed by a spirit of good fun and comedy. In this, of course, it follows the example of Wu Ch'eng-en's novel. C. T. Hsia has said that the *Hsi-yu chi* is a novel of "comic fantasy,"[95] and this description will apply equally well to the *Hsi-yu pu.* Indeed, Tung's novel is filled with a great many kinds of humor, and these vary all the way from the extremely subtle kind, such as most plays on words, to the plain and obvious kind, usually situational, such as, for example, the sequence of scenes in which Monkey acts in disguise as Beauty Yü.

Much of the humor is based either directly or indirectly upon a skillful use of language. For example, the various forms of satire are a kind of humor. Earlier it was mentioned that certain passages of classical prose were written as parodies of accepted literary forms, the best example being the examination essay, which is a parody on the eight-legged essay. The success of the parody is directly dependent upon the ability of the author to adjust his language in such a way as to make the object of his parody appear ridiculous. That is to say, a contrast is implied between the real and the distortion of the real in the parody, and this must be conveyed through a subtle manipulation of language.

Some verse materials also lend themselves to humor. For instance, the lines composed by Monkey in the games he plays with

the three lovely ladies are in the nature of subtle humor. The
following passage will demonstrate this:

There was nothing Monkey could do but lift up his face and think it out.
He engaged in inane thought for a long time and then directing his words
to [the ladies at] the table said, "Let's not have set phrases by the ancients,
all right?" Lady Green [Pearl] said, "You'll have to ask the judge about
this." So then Monkey asked Hsi Shih, and Hsi Shih said, "What hin-
drance is there here? If Beauty produces [a line] then it will be a set line of
the ancients." They all inclined their ears and listened. Monkey then sang
out a line of poetry:

> The repentent heart, following the clouds
> and rain, flies.[96]

The humor here is more apparent in the Chinese than in the English translation, for in the Chinese the words "repentent heart" are
*ch'an-hui-hsin* and these mark the line as clearly Buddhist. Monkey
is unable, despite his disguise, to escape his Buddhist orientation
and one of the ladies soon points out that there is nothing wrong
with his verse except that it carries a monkish flavor.

The above passage also contains a play on the words *ku-jen
ch'eng-chü* (set phrases by the ancients). What is being asked for
here is a matching verse in what the ladies have called the *ku-shih* or
"ancient verse" form. Monkey does not want to use the set phrases
of the ancients because he, not being a poet or scholar, does not
remember any. Hsi Shih jokes about this when she suggests that
whatever Beauty produces will be an ancient verse. After all,
Monkey is disguised as Beauty Yü, who lived at the time of the
founding of the Han dynasty.

CHAPTER 5

# *Narrative Materials (Story) in* Hsi-yu pu

THE *Hsi-yu pu* as a novel is not just language but language which has been put together in such a way as to form a narrative. Here I accept the following definition of narrative, given by Robert Scholes and Robert Kellogg: "By narrative we mean all those literary works which are distinguished by two characteristics: the presence of a story and a story-teller."[1]

It will be convenient to divide the study in this chapter along the lines suggested by this definition, considering first matters related to the storyteller and then those related to his story.

## I *The Storyteller, the Author, and Tradition*

In dealing with the storyteller or narrator it is important first to understand something of his relationship to Tung, the author, and there are two things to be said here. The narrator exists in his own right as a fictional creation of the author. At the same time, however, it appears that Tung identifies himself closely with his narrator.

Modern literary criticism has shown how necessary it is in fiction to recognize that a narrator is to be distinguished from an author. That such a distinction should be made will not be hard to see in the case of a dramatized narrator, for in a certain sense such a narrator often becomes a character almost as vivid as those about whom he narrates. It is in the case of the undramatized narrator where the distinction is often overlooked. Nevertheless, it is still there. Wayne Booth writes:

Even the novel in which no narrator is dramatized creates an implicit picture of an author who stands behind the scenes, whether as stage manager, as puppeteer, or as an indifferent God, silently paring his fingernails.

This implied author is always distinct from the "real man" — whatever we may take him to be — who creates a superior version of himself, a "second self," as he creates his work.[2]

In the *Hsi-yu pu* we do not have a dramatized narrator. The narrator never speaks in the first person and never becomes part of the internal action himself. Yet, he is also quite different from the kind of undramatized narrator of whom Booth speaks and who is characteristic of much modern fiction. He is cast in the role of the traditional Chinese storyteller. As such, we get much more than just an implicit picture of him, for his presence is felt by the reader because of the several traditional modes of narration he uses. However, he is the creation of the author and as such is distinct from the author.

Having recognized the distinction between narrator and author, we are immediately led to the question of distance between the two. Modern Western novelists are not only aware of such a possibility but employ it to their good advantage.[3] No one has yet made a thorough study of how distance operates in traditional Chinese fiction. Potentially, it could shed light on certain problem areas.[4] It should not be assumed, however, that the narrator is *ipso facto* the author himself. I quote Booth again:

In any reading experience there is an implied dialogue among author, narrator, the other characters, and the reader. Each of the four can range, in relation to each of the others, from identification to complete opposition, on any axis of value, moral, intellectual, aesthetic, and even physical.[5]

In the *Hsi-yu pu* the relationship between author and narrator appears to be very close. There is no evidence to suggest significant distance here, for, in Hanan's words, the author "assumes the persona of the public story-teller addressing his audience."[6] The attitudes and beliefs of the storyteller seem to be Tung Yüeh's own.

Not only is the storyteller's relation to the author important, but the author's relationship through his storyteller to a given narrative tradition is also important. By choosing to write his novel in the form of a supplement to the *Hsi-yu chi,* Tung Yüeh chose to write in a well-defined Chinese narrative tradition.

Chinese vernacular narrative, which we are now taking as a form of written narrative, was closely associated in its beginnings with oral narrative. From this it developed roughly in three stages, which followed one after the other but with much overlapping.

The first stage was that of the short story. The earliest examples of vernacular narrative are a kind of story known as *pien-wen*. These were written forms of oral presentations by storytellers of the T'ang dynasty.[7] Later, during the Sung dynasty, as Chinese society became more complex and especially as cities arose, producing a new urban class with its own set of values and interests, oral storytelling became increasingly popular. There are records of professional storytellers complete with classification as to type and references to professional guilds.[8] The storytellers generated a type of short story known as the *hua-pen,* or "story books." These may originally have been used as promptbooks; however, as time went on and as they were passed down, new stories were added which although still bearing the marks of the oral storyteller were now written to be read rather than to be told. The most popular collections of Sung and post-Sung storybooks are the three collections known as the *San-yen.*[9] It is significant to note that these were edited and published by Feng Meng-lung no more than twenty years before Tung Yüeh wrote his novel.[10]

At the same time as the rise and popularity of the short stories another development occurred. Great story cycles were generated, with clusters of stories all centering on certain characters and events, many with some historical foundation. This tendency, of course, was fostered by the practice of the oral storytellers in presenting their materials in consecutive episodes, and also by the practice of organizing themselves in terms of their own specialties. It is from these story cycles that the second stage of the vernacular narrative developed. We may call this the stage of the composite novel. Short stories, of course, continued to be popular, but now in addition to these there appeared the great early vernacular novels. These brought together independently circulating but related short stories, now fashioned into long novels. Such composite novels include not only the *San-kuo chih yen-yi (Romance of the Three Kingdoms)* and the *Shui-hu chuan (Water Margin)* but also the *Hsi-yu chi.*[11]

The third and final stage in the tradition was not reached until the end of the sixteenth century with the appearance of the novel *Chin P'ing Mei* (best known in English translation as *The Golden Lotus*). Here for the first time was a long work which may be called primarily the product of one man's imagination.[12] From this time on there are numerous works which are primarily by single authors.

Thus, the pattern was that of short stories first, followed by composite novels based largely on short-story cycles, and finally single-authorship long novels.

How does the *Hsi-yu pu* relate to this tradition? First, it seems to draw on the short-story tradition. It is much shorter than the standard long novels, having only sixteen chapters, whereas the standard novels are of one hundred chapters or more in length. Also, it is presented as part of a larger cycle of stories connected with the Westward Journey. However, it also reflects aspects of the composite-novel tradition. It is written in the form of a supplement and is supposed to provide one more episode for Wu Ch'eng-en's *Hsi-yu chi*. In this it is similar to the *Chin P'ing Mei,* which also reflects the composite tradition by taking off from one episode in the *Shui-hu chuan.* At the same time the *Hsi-yu pu* also draws on the tradition of the single-authorship long novel. It was written by one man, Tung Yüeh, and it is divided into chapters in the form of a *chang-hui hsiao-shuo* (novel with chapter divisions). Internally, it has its own structure with a sequence of separate episodes. Thus, it may properly be called a novel in its own right. Yet, it must be recognized that in terms of the tradition and especially with reference to the question of genre distinction, the *Hsi-yu pu* presents itself as something of a hybrid.[13]

In looking more closely at the novel, we find that it bears some of the formal characteristics of works in the early tradition. All chapters have subheadings, and in each case the subheading consists of a couplet of seven-syllable lines. The subheadings all contain information pointing toward the contents of the succeeding chapter. Chapters 1 and 2 begin with short prologues. In Chapter 1 this consists of a seven-syllable quatrain which is important in setting the theme not only for the chapter but for the whole novel, and this is followed by a statement in prose explicating the theme. In the second chapter, the prologue is also thematic, consisting of a seven-syllable couplet.

What is significant is that after the second chapter there are no more chapter prologues. In fact, with only one exception, there are no more overt storyteller intrusions to mark chapter divisions. Chapters simply follow one on the other in a continuous narrative flow, with only the chapter numbers and their subheadings to serve as divisions. The one exception mentioned comes at the end of Chapter 12, where we read:

A vague fire began to burn [within Monkey]. His anger mounted by degree. With all his heart he just wanted to kill Prince Little Moon and so get to see the matter clearly. If you don't know how it finally turned out, you may listen to the explanation in the next chapter.[14]

This represents one instance in which Tung was following the old vernacular tradition based on the oral performance. Significantly, the last sentence above, which embodies this tradition, has been edited out of the recent Commercial Press punctuated edition.

Further remnants of the early tradition may be seen in the regular use of what Cyril Birch calls "story-teller phrases."[15] Such formal characteristics are hardly worth mentioning in themselves, for they are simply part of the early tradition and may be found in all the standard works, including the *Hsi-yu chi*. What is significant, however, is that there are so few direct references by the storyteller to his audience. Such references are conspicuous in Tung's novel only by their absence. Furthermore, the few remnants of the oral tradition which do exist suggest, as does the example given above, that Tung was attempting to break from the tradition. His work was written to be read, and elements which could only serve a useful function in an oral situation were eliminated. Tung's storyteller found himself being pushed into the background. Of course, the tradition persisted in spite of Tung. As far as formulaic chapter endings are concerned, these were still observed even in such late novels as the *Hung-lou meng (Dream of the Red Chamber)* and the *Lao-ts'an yu chi (Travels of Lao Ts'an)*.

## II  *The Storyteller and His Techniques*

An analysis of the techniques used by Tung's storyteller indicates that, in general, they are of the traditional kind. Tung's storyteller may have been receding into the background, but his basic method of narration had not changed.

A useful scheme proposed by Hanan for analyzing the technique of vernacular narrative will be used here. Hanan distinguishes three distinct modes of narration.[16] The first is the mode of commentary, and this appears in several ways. The two formal elements mentioned above of subheadings and prologues are frequent vehicles for commentary. A chapter subheading generally puts into capsulized form the content of the chapter to follow. A good example of this is the subheading for Chapter 2, which reads:

A New T'ang is conjured up on the road to the West,
And a splendid Son of Heaven appears in the Green
    Jade Hall.[17]

Through the subheading the narrator prepares the reader for
what will follow, but sometimes the subheading does more than
just summarize. It may provide vital information which if missed
may lead to a misunderstanding of the story. An example of this
comes in the subheading to the first chapter, where we read:

When the peonies are red the Mackerel casts his spell,[18]
And after delivering his text of grievances the
    Great Sage is detained.[19]

This and the reference in the prologue to the chapter are the only
times the Mackerel and his spell are mentioned until the last chapter. Therefore, it is vital to the reader that he understand what the
narrator is telling him here so that he can pick up the theme as it is
drawn out indirectly later. The prologues function in a similar way,
although there are only two of them in the novel.

Frequently passages of commentary are connected with
Monkey's character. For instance, after the killing of the women
and children we are told of Monkey that, "in fact, although Great
Sage Sun could fight bravely, by nature he was kind and benevolent."[20] In the second chapter, when Monkey goes to Heaven and
finds that the gate is shut and he cannot get in, the narrator en-
lightens us by saying, "He [Monkey] was a hot-tempered person
and impatient by nature. How could he endure interminable
rebuke?"[21] More examples could be given but none that would vary
greatly from this pattern. The narrator shows remarkable restraint
in overt manipulation of his story. When he does intrude directly it
is usually for short comments. Frequently, as in the first quotation
on Monkey above, passages of commentary are introduced by *yüan
lai* (in fact).

A second mode is that of description, and descriptive passages
are easily identified in three ways. They are, of course, set off first
by their content, but this is not all. They are also usually introduced
by terms such as *tan chien* or *chih chien* (all one can see is...).
Finally, their form is usually distinctive. As Hanan says, "The
description is usually cast into the form of a passage of parallel
prose, full of stereotyped, classical language and rather overblown

imagery."[22] And so, for instance, we have a passage describing the three beauties on the Grasping Incense Terrace.[23] Or again, we have in Chapter 15 an elaborate description, partly in parallel prose, of military troops lined up for roll call.[24]

The third mode is that of presentation. Here the storyteller keeps his own personality as much as possible out of the narration and proceeds with his passages of dialogue and action. In the case of the *Hsi-yu pu,* the main portion of the novel is in this mode. Usually presentation is introduced by such standard storyteller phrases as *hua shuo* (it is told how), *ch'ieh shuo* (and now we tell how), and *ch'üeh shuo* (but now we tell how). This mode best gives the illusion of objectivity, for the storyteller can never completely remove himself from his story. And, of course, behind the storyteller is the author, and as Booth has pointed out, "the author's judgment is always present, always evident to anyone who knows how to look for it."[25]

It may be said that the mode of presentation is one of showing rather than telling. Thus, in the very first chapter, after the prologue, in which the narrator tells us the gist of what is to follow, he shows us what happens after the Monk and his disciples leave Flaming Mountain. We are shown how Monkey is susceptible to the Mackerel's spell. When the dream commences, we are shown how confused Monkey is by being allowed to enter his own thought processes. The whole dream itself, in which Monkey has one strange experience after another, is an attempt to show what it is like to be in a state of illusion. The ending of the illusion comes dramatically when we are shown how Monkey slays the Mackerel monster. In looking at the novel as a whole, it is surprising how much Tung's storyteller has been able to convey just by means of this mode of presentation.

In addition to these three modes, Tung's storyteller uses two basic kinds of narration, which may conveniently be called direct narration and indirect narration. In direct narration it is the storyteller himself who does the narrating; in indirect narration he uses a character in his story for this purpose. I shall call this character the narrator-agent.[26] A narrator-agent is, in fact, a kind of dramatized narrator, but insofar as the information he provides lies within the scope of what is being presented by the principal narrator he serves as an agent.

In the second chapter Monkey, now dreaming, comes upon the New T'ang, and after an unsuccessful attempt to enter Heaven to

gain an explanation for this phenomenon, he returns and enters the
strange land. At the gate he is warned regarding his own safety.
Then he changes into a butterfly and flits around, meanwhile
observing the splendor everywhere. Finally, he comes to rest on top
of a great hall below the Wu-hua Lou (Tower of Five Flowers). He
reads inscriptions above the gate of the hall and also on its walls, all
the while learning more about this peculiar place. He makes a comment to himself regarding the last inscription and then we read:

As he [Monkey] finished talking [to himself], suddenly a palace servant
walked out. In her hand she held a broom of green bamboo and as she
swept the ground she spoke to herself and said, "Ha! Ha! The emperor is
asleep and the chief ministers are asleep. The Green Jade Hall has now
become a pavilion of sleeping immortals. Our romantic Son of Heaven
spent last night with Ch'ing-kuo Fu-jen (Lady Overthrower of
States)...."[27]

There then follows a long passage of uninterrupted narration by
this palace servant. Not only is the emperor described in terms of
his relations to his ladies, but the palace servant adds some of her
own experiences and draws her own conclusions about it all. This
passage is humorous, satirical, and it bolsters the central theme of
the novel. In terms of narrative technique, it is an example of the
narrator telling his story indirectly through a narrator-agent.
Furthermore, the agent herself uses all three modes of narration.

In the third chapter, Monkey has overheard the deliberations carried on by the emperor and his ministers. The decision has been
made to recall the T'ang Monk with the offer of a general's com-
mission. The messenger leaves and Monkey follows him out but is
unable to overtake him. Then Monkey comes upon an incredible
scene. Ahead of him are a group of spacewalkers hacking away at
the sky. Quite perplexed at this unusual sight,

Monkey then called out to the head officer of the sky-hackers, "Under the
command of what prince are you? Why are you carrying on this strange
business?" They all put down their axes and saluted in space. He [the head
officer[ then said, "Honorable Tung-nan Chang-lao (Elder in the Southeast, i.e., Monkey), as a tribe we are called 'the spacewalkers' and we live
in Chin-li Ts'un (Gold Carp Village)...."[28]

Here again a long passage of narration follows, with the space-
walker providing Monkey and more importantly the reader with

important information. In the course of his explanations as to why the spacewalkers are hacking at the sky, Prince Little Moon and the Green, Green World are first introduced.

Indirect narration serves two functions. First, with it the narrator is able to provide the reader with readily assimilated information. Since the material is presented in dialogue, it is compact in form and the narrator may use it for any number of purposes. Yet, it is told by a person in the story, a dramatized narrator, and so it serves the second function of relieving the main narrator of the work of narration. Of course, he has introduced his own narrator-agent. The author is merely using an indirect method in telling his story.

## III  *The Story and External Continuity*

The story in the *Hsi-yu pu* forces us to look in two different directions. It is both a supplement which assumes an external continuity and an independent work with its own internal coherence and unity.

As has been indicated in the Introduction, the novel supplements Wu Ch'eng-en's *Hsi-yu chi*. Furthermore, it is made quite clear just where the supplement is to fit. Immediately after the prologue to the first chapter the story proper begins with these words, "It is told that after the T'ang Monk and his three disciples left Flaming Mountain, days and months came and went and then it was springtime again."[29] Wu's novel was written in one hundred chapters, which Hu Shih has divided into the following three parts: the first seven chapters contain the story of Monkey; Chapters 8 through 12 contain the story of Hsüan Tsang and the origin of the mission to India; and Chapters 13 through 100 contain the story of the pilgrimage itself.[30] The pilgrimage is built around a sequence of eighty-one trials, all but the last occurring prior to arrival in the Western Paradise. Among these is the episode connected with Flaming Mountain, which is described in Chapters 59 through 61. Tung's novel, as a supplement, begins with this episode.

The matter of continuity may be studied in a number of ways. First, there is general continuity with everything in the former novel occurring through Chapter 61. Tung was obviously quite familiar with Wu's work and establishes many links with it. A few examples will be examined.

In Chapter 1, just before Monkey sets out to beg for alms, he returns to the peonies and teases the sleeping Pigsy. Impersonating the T'ang Monk, he tells how the Bodhisattva has just passed by and said of Pigsy, "Wu-neng (Aware of Ability), who is so fond of sleeping, can't make it up the Western Paradise either. You give him this message. Tell him to go and marry Chen'chen (Truth), Ai-ai (Love), and Lien-lien (Affection)."[31] The reference is to the three goddesses who in the former novel had transformed themselves into beautiful girls and offered themselves to Pigsy as a temptation.[32] On several occasions when Monkey in his dream is especially hard pressed, he takes the form used when earlier he created the disturbance in Heaven.[33] This refers to Monkey's riotous behavior in Heaven in the former novel.[34] At the end of Chapter 7 and the beginning of Chapter 8, Monkey meets the Liu Tsei (Six Thieves). He is in disguise as Beauty Yü, and as they are trying to rob him he changes back into his normal form and slays them.[35] These thieves are the same ones met in the former novel where, when they threatened the Monk, Monkey slew them.[36] Liu Po-ch'in, the man who appears to Monkey in the mirror in Chapter 4,[37] is the same Liu Po-ch'in of the former novel.[38] When in Chapter 15 Monkey joins the army, he joins as his own double named Liu-erh Mi-hou (Six-Eared Ape).[39] This ape was one who as Monkey's double created much confusion earlier on the journey.[40]

Of course, general continuity is not achieved just by such specific links but more especially through the fact that the whole setting is that of the former novel. The characters in the basic story are the same and there is continuity in their personalities and characteristics.

In addition to general continuity there is also specific continuity, that is, continuity with reference to the exact place where the supplement fits. It is not by chance that the *Hsi-yu pu* takes up after the Flaming Mountain episode.

In this episode the Monk and his disciples are prevented from continuing westward by coming upon a mountain enveloped in flames, which can only be extinguished with a certain magic palm leaf fan which happens to be in the possession of Lo-ch'a Nü (Madam Raksasa), the T'ieh-shan Hsien (Iron Fan Immortal). Since the pilgrims must cross the mountain, it is imperative that they get the fan and put out the flames. The three chapters which recount this episode tell of Monkey's three successive attempts to get the magic fan. First, when Monkey approaches Madam Raksasa she refuses to give him the fan, and so he changes into an insect and is swallowed by the lady as she drinks her tea. Inside her stomach, Monkey thrashes about, causing her such discomfort that she finally agrees to turn over the fan. When she does so, however, it turns out to be an imitation and does not work. For Monkey's second attempt he changes into Niu-mo Wang (Bull Monster King), Madam Raksasa's husband, and she receives him without suspicion. She has been separated from her husband for two years and thinking that he has now returned, serves wine to celebrate. Soon she is half-drunk and also sexually aroused, and it is clear that Monkey is either led to compromise his chastity or at least is sorely tempted to do so. His deception, however, works, for not only does he get the real fan but also is told how to use it. He then escapes, but before he can use the fan he is overtaken by Bull Monster King, now in disguise as Pigsy. This time it is Monkey's turn to be tricked, and without any suspicion he hands the fan over to Bull Monster King when asked for it. The third attempt involves a fierce battle in which a great number of heavenly forces intervene on Monkey's side. Monkey is now victorious, puts out the flames, and so the pilgrims cross the mountain and proceed westward.

The specific point of continuity comes in reference to Monkey's relations with Madam Raksasa. He has shown his vulnerability to worldly temptation and Tung begins his supplement at this point to demonstrate this fact. The link with the lady, although hinted at throughout the whole novel, is not brought out directly until the very end of Monkey's dream. In a great climactic battle, Monkey meets Po-lo-mi Wang (Prince Paramita), who turns out to be his own son. Paramita tells his story and says:

Later he [Monkey] changed into a little insect and worked his way into my mother's stomach. He stayed there for a long time thrashing around unceasingly. My mother then could bear it no longer and had to give the palm leaf fan to my father, Monkey. My father, Monkey, took the palm leaf fan, fanned and cooled Flaming Mountain and then finally left. By the fifth month of the next year my mother, all of a sudden, gave birth to me, Prince Paramita.[41]

In the dream, conception is believed to taken place when Monkey was in the form of an insect in Madam Raksasa's stomach rather than when Monkey, in his second attempt, dallied with the amorous lady while disguised as her husband. Since this is Monkey's dream, Tung may be suggesting that Monkey was inexperienced and consequently ignorant in sexual matters. In any case, there is specific continuity here between the supplement and the immediately preceding episode in the *Hsi-yu chi*.

Finally, external continuity may be seen in the episodic nature of Tung's novel. It assumes not only what precedes but also what follows, for no attempt is made to provide an ending for the Westward Journey. Also, the pattern of the story fits the standard pattern of the former novel. The Mackerel Spirit is just another monster among the many already encountered, and this episode takes its place along with all the other episodes. As the narrator tells us:

> In fact, the Mackerel Spirit confused the mental monkey (*hsin-yüan*) just so that he could eat the flesh of the T'ang Monk. Therefore, on one hand he bedeviled the Great Sage and on the other hand took on the form of a little monk to beguile the T'ang monk.[42]

This is the basic pattern. Tripitaka is presented as a monk so holy that any monster lucky enough to eat his flesh or drink his semen is assured of immortality. As T. A. Hsia points out, what marks the difference in the case of the Mackerel is that now we have a monster whose strategy is to dispose of Monkey first and then to get at the Monk.[43]

## IV   *The Story and Internal Unity*

Although there is external continuity, in a real sense the novel may also be said to be self-contained. As a single episode on the Westward Journey, it has its own unity and this may easily be demonstrated by outlining the basic story.

The story is divided into three parts. The first chapter comprises the introduction and the last chapter the conclusion and what lies in between is Monkey's dream. Essentially then it is the account of a dream to which an introduction and a conclusion have been added. The introduction constitutes the setting with its link to the Flaming Mountain episode and provides a thematic rationale for the dream. The conclusion brings Monkey out of his dream, provides further thematic explanation, and then offers a final resolution in the slaying of the fish monster. The story is self-contained in that at the end we are brought right back again to where we were in the beginning, with the one difference being that presumably we now have a wiser Monkey.

Here two questions need to be taken up. The first is whether or not what we have in Chapters 2 through 15 is a dream at all. Nowhere does Tung tell us that Monkey is entering a dream world. The strange world of illusions is simply introduced. The first chapter does, however, offer clues suggesting that what follows is a dream. In the prologue we are told that Monkey will see that the sources of "worldly desires are but floating clouds and dreamy illusions."[44] Coupled with this is the first line of the subheading of the last chapter, which reads, "The Venerable One of the Void calls the ape from his dream,"[45] and also the corresponding passage in the same chapter, in which the Venerable One does call Monkey and then says to him, "By this time haven't you awakened yet?"[46] Also, in the thirteenth chapter, when Monkey finds himself especially confused as he views Prince Little Moon and the T'ang Monk enjoying themselves together, he asks, "Could it be that Old Sun is having a dream?"[47] Of course, it could be argued that the word "dream" is used here metaphorically. We are dealing with a fictional Monkey and a supernatural one at that. However, the author clearly intends to show us that Monkey has a prolonged illusory experience and insofar as it is similar to dreams as we know them, we may conveniently call it such.

A second question is that of when the dream actually starts. Was Monkey already in a dream state in the first chapter? He certainly was already under the spell of the Mackerel. One commentator obviously sees no break in continuity between the first and second chapters when he writes:

The first time Monkey entered the demonic was with the boys and girls of spring. The second time he entered the demonic was on the Grasping Incense Terrace.[48]

The commentator here speaks in the context of desire as sexual attraction, but the point is that he makes no distinction between the first and second chapters in terms of the illusory experience.

It appears, however, that for the sake of consistency of narrative point of view in the first and the last chapters it is necessary to take the experiences in both as outside of the dream proper. At the end of the first chapter Monkey returns to the peonies and finds the Master and the other disciples asleep. In the last chapter, after Monkey is awakened from his dream, he is blown back to where the peonies are. At the same time we are told that the Monk awakens from his sleep and notices that the boys and girls who were teasing him have long since dispersed. Obviously, then, in the last chapter the Monk's earlier experience with the boys and girls and his subsequent falling asleep are not taken as part of Monkey's dream. Since these events occurred in the first chapter, they must be taken as outside the dream there as well. Thus, we see the dream proper beginning with the second chapter and running through the fifteenth chapter.

In considering internal unity and coherence there are two levels which must be kept distinct. The first is that which characterizes the relationship between the three main parts of the novel as outlined above; the second is in connection with the dream itself.

The dream consists of a series of episodes, many of which are of a highly unusual nature, and these may usefully be organized into four sequential clusters. The word "cluster" seems appropriate because in each case there is one central experience around which a number of episodes revolves. The relationship between individual episodes and this central experience varies. Sometimes it is clear, but at other times it is ambiguous, where several possible relationships exist. The four clusters are:

1. Episodes in Chapters 2 and 3 focusing on Monkey's experiences in the New T'ang.
2. Episodes in Chapters 4 through 7 focusing on Monkey's experiences in the World of the Ancients.
3. Episodes in Chapters 8 and 9 focusing on Monkey's experiences in the World of the Future.
4. Episodes in Chapters 10 through 15 focusing on Monkey's experiences in the Green, Green World proper.

At the level of the dream, unity and coherence are not found on the same terms as with the basic structure of the novel itself. This may seem obvious, and yet it is important to observe, for it suggests the technique whereby Tung creates the complex world of the novel. It is the technique of presenting an illusory experience in which unity and coherence are found not within the rational requirements of conscious experience but through a set of symbols, the meanings of which support a central theme. Thus, in terms of narrative structure, we can outline the dream as clusters of episodes, but the unity and coherence by which these clusters are related can only be understood by a careful study of theme.

The dream as a creation of illusion serves its function well. Through it the author attains great freedom. He is not bound by the limits of conscious logic and in this case not even by the logic of the world of the *Hsi-yu chi*. This allows him full use of his powers of imagination, and he is able not only to explore subtle areas of human experience but also to create a world of meaning remarkable in its complexity.

## CHAPTER 6

# Conceptual Materials (Theme) in
# Hsi-yu pu

A third category of significant materials are those which may be called "conceptual." The term is not used here in the broad sense to include all ideas in any way associated with the *Hsi-yu pu,* but rather in a narrow sense to mean specifically those ideas used by Tung Yüeh to develop his theme. Indeed, many ideas are suggested by the novel which are not, strictly speaking, a part of its theme. Some of these are important for understanding the world of the novel and will be taken up later. The conceptual materials of the theme are separate from these. They are interrelated, form a clear pattern, and should be considered together.

## I  *The Didactic Nature of the Theme*

Thematically, the *Hsi-yu pu* may be categorized as a Buddhist fable. Of course, such categorization runs the risk of distortion by taking a term from the Western literary tradition and applying it to a work not of this tradition. Yet, the limitations of language are such that this risk can hardly be avoided, and what seems to be necessary is careful attention to definition.

Fable is used here in the sense of didactic fiction, and in this sense its meaning is considerably broader than commonly understood. Beckson and Ganz define fable as:

A brief narrative, in either verse or prose, which illustrates some moral truth. The characters are often animals, as in the fables attributed to the Greek slave Aesop, but are not invariably so.[1]

This is the common definition, and it will be noted that it includes brevity of narrative and didactic motivation. The broader definition of fable as didactic fiction frees it of the limitation of brevity while retaining its didactic motivation.

To understand this it is necessary not only to distinguish fable from the common definition but to understand what is meant by didactic fiction. Here I draw on the general theory of types of narrative as developed by Scholes and Kellogg.[2] These two critics make a distinction between empirical narrative and fictional narrative. The two types are antithetical, with empirical narrative stressing allegiance to reality and fictional narrative stressing allegiance to an ideal. Empirical narrative is further subdivided into the historical and the mimetic, and fictional narrative into the romantic and the didactic. It is didactic fiction in this sense which is understood as fable. I quote from Scholes and Kellogg:

> The didactic subdivision of fiction we may call *fable,* a form which is ruled by an intellectual and moral impulse as romance is ruled by an esthetic one. The human intellect being what it is, fable tends toward brevity in narrative, and is inclined to lean heavily on romance for narrative articulation if the narrative artist has anything like a sustained flight in mind.[3]

Tung's novel, with its strong thematic thrust, fits this definition. It is fictional in the sense that its allegiance is to an ideal rather than to reality, and the ideal in its broadest sense is the Buddhist view of life. The theme of the novel is built around this ideal and it is in itself didactic in tone. The intention of the author is to promote the Buddhist view through his theme. Of course, this is not the author's only intention, for he is also motivated aesthetically. However, this is his intention insofar as the theme is concerned, and since the narrative is sustained over sixteen chapters the tendency pointed out by Scholes and Kellogg for longer fables to "lean heavily on romance for narrative articulation" is clearly present. There is a constant mixing of romance with fable, of aesthetic concerns with didactic concerns. In terms of thematic concepts, however, the didactic dominates.

The question of why the theme is not simply described as a Buddhist allegory now arises. The answer lies in the complexity of the novel. A careful study of the world of the novel will show that it may be taken at no less than three different levels, and this means that various thematic elements are best seen symbolically, not allegorically. For instance, Monkey, the hero, may stand either for man as a dreamer, or for man facing the evils of late Ming society, or for man as a member of the human race. Most likely he stands for all three and is thus symbolic. Here we make a distinction between symbolism and allegory which has been summarized by Professor James J. Y. Liu as follows:

> The main difference between symbolism and allegory is easy to perceive. In allegory, there is no difficulty in identifying "what represents" with "what is represented." Indeed, allegory usually consists of personifications of specific virtues and vices (such as in Spenser's *Faerie Queene*), or the reverse — representations of actual persons or institutions in the guise of non-human beings (such as in Dryden's *The Hind and the Panther*). In symbolism, as I mentioned once before, it is not always possible to name what is represented. In other words, a symbol is capable of several interpretations, some of which may be simultaneously acceptable. That is why symbolism has greater richness and subtlety of meaning than allegory.[4]

As I have already shown, there is an allegorical scheme in Tung's novel, with words sounding like *ch'ing* standing for desire.[5] Yet in a work as complex as the *Hsi-yu pu,* one must avoid the temptation to rush in with full-blown allegorical interpretations, for these can only preclude the possibility of multileveled meanings. Unless, of course, the author himself or some other reliable source tells us so, allegory should only be identified as such when two criteria are met. The first is that identification should come from within the work itself. That is to say, one must not start with an allegorical scheme externally derived and then try to force the imagery into this scheme. Second, the work may be seen as allegorical only in the absence of other valid interpretations. In short, allegorical interpretation is flat and one-dimensional. The more complex a work of literary art is in terms of subtlety of meaning the less likelihood there is for allegory.

## II   *The Theme Introduced*

Conceptual materials in the *Hsi-yu pu* are closely related to and interwoven with the narrative. The two sets of materials, the narrative and the conceptual, go together, each reinforcing the other, and it is only for analytical purposes that they are separated. Just as the story may be outlined in terms of three parts, with an introduction, the dream, and a conclusion, so also may the theme be shown to develop in three stages.

The first chapter contains the thematic introduction and itself may be divided into three parts, a thematic statement plus two supporting episodes. The thematic statement is the subheading to the first chapter plus its prologue. In the subheading we learn that there is a Ch'ing-yü (Mackerel), and thus the author presents at the very outset his allegorical scheme on *ch'ing*. Also we learn that the redness of the peonies is to be associated with this Mackerel and that Monkey is going to be involved somehow in the Mackerel's breath (*ch'i*), or as I have translated it, "spell."[6]

Immediately following the subheading, an old quatrain is quoted which reads:

All things from the beginning have had just one body,
   Yet this body contains the cosmic duality.[7]
We dare to open clear eyes for the finite world,
   And turn our backs [on the view that] rivers
   and mountains are separately established.[8]

This verse provides the philosophical basis for the theme that although there is a cosmic duality in the world it resolves itself into a final unity and both man and nature find a common source in this. The unity of the single body is what is important. Following the quatrain comes the explanatory sentence of the prologue, which reads:

In this chapter the Mackerel stirs up trouble, confusing the Mental Monkey, so that in the end it will be seen that the causes of worldly desires are but floating clouds and dream illusions.[9]

The theme is now fully stated in all its simplicity. Worldly desires as represented by the Mackerel will cause Monkey to be confused. The lesson he will learn is that, in view of the nature of cosmic unity, these desires and their consequences are all illusory.

Two episodes follow, and both function as elucidation. The first is Monkey's experience of the peonies and his resulting dispute with Tripitaka. As the group travels along, Monkey sees ahead a grove of beautiful red peonies. He mentions this to the Monk, who thereupon points out that it is not the peonies that are red. This leads to a disagreement between Master and disciple which goes unresolved and only terminates with the Monk's recitation of the following *gatha:*

It isn't the peonies that are red,
But the mind of the disciple that is red.
When all the flowers of the peonies have fallen,
It will be just as before they had opened. [10]

From this episode and the reference to the peonies in the chapter subheading we know that Monkey is already under the influence of the Mackerel, which is to say, under the influence of worldly desire. It is this desire which not only causes him to see the redness which is illusory but also leads to his argument with Tripitaka.

A second episode further elucidates the theme. This is the one concerning the young women and their children, and it serves two functions. First, it contrasts the increasing atmosphere of illusion with the purity of the Monk, this time by setting the children off against the Monk. The children tease Tripitaka about the robe he is wearing. It is a robe of only one color. They ask him for it, and then tell him that if he refuses to give it to them they will go home and ask their mothers to make for them one of many colors. Here twenty-five colors are listed, and we have a striking example of Tung's ability to give free rein to his imagination by producing a string of free-associational images. [11] The images are used for more than just verbal decoration, however, for they suggest the whole range of human desires. Notice the prominence of the color green in "green duck weed," "green willows," "green lotuses," "the color of green," etc., all of which call to mind the allegory on *ch'ing*. Furthermore, willows suggest the pain of parting, the one-winged conjugal birds suggest marital love, the silver seals tied with green ribbons suggest success in the official world, etc. By contrasting the many-colored robe which the children want with the one-colored robe of the Monk, Tung gives a contrast between the illusory world of sensual desire and the transcendent world of the Buddha.

This episode serves a second purpose, which is to show how deeply infected Monkey has become with human desire. In a fit of rage Monkey kills all the women and children, which shows his susceptibility to the emotion of anger. But, no sooner has he finished his slaughter than we find him filled with intense remorse.

Although Great Sage Sun was in fact brave in fighting, yet by nature he was kind and benevolent. As he put his cudgel back behind his ear, quite unaware of it, tears flowed from his eyes. He complained and grumbled at himself, saying, "Heaven! Heaven! I, Wu-k'ung, since my conversion to the Buddhist way, have stilled my emotions and controlled my temper and have never recklessly killed a person. But today I suddenly became terribly angry and destroyed more than fifty people both old and young, boys and girls, and they weren't monsters or bandits. I have forgotten that this is a serious crime indeed."[12]

His remorse leads him to compose a prayer to the souls of those whom he has killed. He further hopes in this way to deceive the Monk into believing that a monster has done the killing and thus avoid punishment for it. When he returns to the peonies he finds that the Monk and the other disciples have fallen asleep, and after playing a joke on Pigsy he sets off, ostensibly to beg for alms.

### III   *The Theme in the Dream*

I have already shown that Monkey's dream covers Chapters 2 through 15, and that in terms of narrative the dream may be outlined as a series of four clusters of episodes centering on four main experiences. These are the experience of the New T'ang, the experience of the World of the Ancients, the experience of the World of the Future, and the experience of the Green, Green World proper.

The question now is how this outline relates to the novel as a Buddhist fable. In what way does the dream bear out the didactic purpose of the author as expressed in the first chapter?

Because of his weakness as revealed in the Flaming Mountain episode of the former novel, Monkey is susceptible to the spell of the Mackerel, who stands for worldly desire. By succumbing to desire, Monkey is led into a realm of illusion, namely, his dream. Examination of the clusters of episodes will furthermore show that they embody two dynamic movements, both of which are directly related to the idea of illusion.

The first such movement is that in the dream Monkey is drawn closer by stages to Prince Little Moon and his Green, Green World. This is important to the basic allegory on *ch'ing,* for it will be recalled that the three Chinese characters for Prince Little Moon combine to form the character for desire.[13] Also, the Green, Green World carries the allegory in the word for green in its name, which is also *ch'ing.* The reduplication of the word intensifies the meaning, and the author appears to be suggesting that the Prince and his world stand for the very essence of desire. As Monkey moves toward these two, he is in effect moving ever nearer to this essence and is thus moving ever deeper into illusion.

The movement may be seen in Monkey's dream experiences. In the first cluster of episodes, Monkey does not even know about the Prince and his world. It is only when Monkey speaks with the spacewalkers that he, as well as the reader, learns of the existence of this strange character. The spacewalkers tell Monkey that the Monk is with the Prince, and this serves as the impetus for Monkey to seek him out. In the second and third clusters, Monkey moves closer to this personification of desire by actually entering his Green, Green World. Yet, Monkey only enters two of the mirrors in its Tower of Myriad Mirrors and thus still remains outside the world proper. The emphasis on the time factor with the World of the Ancients and the World of the Future stresses the idea of distance. Not until the fourth cluster does Monkey really explore the Green, Green World and see the Prince in person.

The second movement runs parallel to the first and is related to it. Not only does Monkey in the dream move closer to the symbolic essence of desire, but he also is by stages confronted with characters who are more closely involved with him personally. In the first cluster the people he sees are nearly all strangers to him. When he visits the World of the Ancients and the World of the Future, the people he meets there are not strangers, for most are well known to him through Chinese history and tradition. Both Monkey and the reader are familiar with Hsi Shih, Hsiang Yü, Ch'in Kuei, and Yüeh Fei. In the last cluster, Monkey meets those individuals most closely involved with him personally. He sees his Master, the Monk, although he is now a layman and quite changed in appearance and attitude. He also sees his fellow disciples Pigsy and Sandy, and finally at the very end he is confronted with Prince Paramita, who turns out to be his own son.

This dual movement toward desire and its heightened illusion on one hand and toward personal involvement on the other is well epitomized in the strange episode in which Monkey visits the old Taoist in his Green Bamboo Cave. What we should note here first is the repeated contrast between nature and the human world. As Monkey and the Taoist walk together to the cave the scenery along the way is described. For example, they come to a place surrounded by a hundred peaks which appear in the most peculiar shapes. Some seem to be gazing up, as if looking at the sky, and others kneeling, as if drinking water. Some seem to be running, some

sleeping, and some whistling. Some appear as scholars sitting opposite each other. Some look as if they were flying, and others seem to
be dancing like ghosts and spirits. Some look like cows, horses, and
sheep.[14] To Monkey it looks like a graveyard with only the tomb-
stones lacking. Here the contrast drawn between nature and the
human world enhances the idea of illusion. It is also notable that in
this episode Monkey has his own fortune told. He is asked to give
that which is most intimate to him, namely, the cyclical characters
for the time and date of his birth. On the basis of these data, the
Taoist predicts his future, which includes his marriage, his acquir-
ing someone (possibly a new master), that he will kill a man, and
his death.[15] The function of this episode is to emphasize the two
movements toward illusion and toward personal involvement.

Monkey is led more and more into a crisis of anxiety. Indeed,
anxiety is a mark of the whole dream, but it reaches its climax at the
very end when Monkey meets his self-proclaimed son, and his son
then proceeds to slay both the Monk and the Prince. The utter confusion of the ensuing battle reflects the unbearable situation in
Monkey's mind, and it is at this point that he is awakened.

## IV   *The Theme Concluded*

The awakening from the dream marks the beginning of the
thematic conclusion. This comes in the last chapter and is developed in three parts. First, there is Monkey's encounter with the
Buddha, the Venerable One of the Void (or Master of the Void).
The Buddha calls out to Monkey, "Wu-k'ung is not aware of
vacuity. Wu-huan is not aware of illusion."[16] Monkey turns around
and asks who it is. He then sees that it is the Buddha sitting on a
lotus platform. The Buddha introduces himself, saying that he has
come to call Monkey from the false world. Then the Buddha
explains all about the Mackerel and his spell.

The Master of the Void said, "Wu-k'ung, you were just now under the
spell of the Mackerel and were bedeviled by him."[17]
   Monkey then asked, "What kind of a demon spirit is the Mackerel that
he can create a whole world?"
   The Master of the Void said, "When Heaven and earth first opened up,
that which was clear went upward and that which was muddy went down-
ward. There was a certain kind which was half clear and half muddy which
went to the middle and this was mankind. There was a certain kind with a

greater portion clear and a lesser portion muddy which went to the Hua-kuo Shan (Mountain of Flowers and Fruit), and which gave birth to Wu-k'ung.[18] There was a certain kind with a greater portion muddy and a lesser portion clear which went to Hsiao-yüeh Tung (Little Moon Cave), and this gave birth to the Mackerel.[19] The Mackerel and Wu-k'ung were born at the same time, on the same day, in the same month, and in the same year. But Wu-k'ung belonged to the good whereas the Mackerel belonged to the bad. Yet in his (the Mackerel's) magic power, he excelled over Wu-k'ung by tenfold. Furthermore, his body grew to be especially large, so that when his head rested on the K'un-lun Shan (K'un-lun Mountain),[20] his feet were on Yu-mi Kuo (Land of Obscurity and Confusion).[21] Now the world of the real part was narrow and small, and so he lived in the illusory part, himself calling it the Green, Green World."

Monkey said, "What is the illusory part and what the real part?"

The Master said, "Creation has three parts: the nonillusory part, the illusory part, and the real part."[22]

The Buddha recites a *gatha* to further explain that Monkey's illusory experience was all self-induced, and then a strong gust of wind blows Monkey back to the peonies again. This encounter with the Buddha provides an important explanation as to the origin and nature of the Mackerel. This fish has not been mentioned since the first chapter, and there only in the prologue. The reader now at last knows who the fish is and just what he has done, and the thematic meaning of the dream is clarified. Also, with the reference to the three portions of creation, a metaphysical foundation for the theme is given.

The second part of the conclusion contains the Mackerel's attempt to deceive Tripitaka by presenting a new disciple to him. This is immediately followed by commentary from the narrator:

In fact, the Mackerel Spirit deluded the Mental Monkey just in order to eat the flesh of the T'ang Monk. Therefore, on one hand he befuddled the Great Sage and on the other hand he disguised himself in the form of a little monk, playing a trick on the T'ang Monk. Who would have known that the Great Sage would be awakened by the Venerable One of the Void? Truly,

> Monsters and wicked ones may exhaust a thousand schemes,
> But one whose mind is right has never had to fear the demons.[23]

Upon his return Monkey immediately detects the evil aura surrounding the new disciple and knows that this is the Mackerel in disguise. He then slays the monster. This episode provides in dramatic form a reinforcement of the thematic conclusion. We know that Monkey has been awakened from the delusion of his dream, and since the dream was self-induced, his enlightenment implies the destruction of the cause of the delusion. The slaying of the fish serves as a dramatic enactment of this conclusion. Of course, it also serves as part of the narrative in that it is the conclusion to the part played by the fish in the story.

There is yet a third part to the thematic conclusion. Monkey is sent off for food. He first meets the earth god, who explains why he could not help when called upon to do so earlier.[24] Monkey goes on, but instead of finding food he sees a village.

Monkey ran on in and was just about to look for someone from whom to beg food when suddenly he came upon a quiet hut. Inside the quiet hut there sat a teacher who was lecturing on a book with several disciples gathered around him. What sentence do you think he was lecturing on? He was just lecturing on the sentence, "Its scope includes Heaven and earth and so it is not in error."[25]

We have observed with what great care Tung introduced his theme in the first chapter. It is with equal care that he concludes it in the last chapter. By introducing the Venerable One of the Void, he makes possible an explanation for the fish spirit and the dream. Although the essentials of the theme were stated in the first chapter, much was left unsaid. The mackerel was never explained nor a reason given for the dream, and this served to generate some suspense throughout the novel. Now, with the Venerable One of the Void and his explanation, the suspense is resolved. However, this is not all. Having effected a thematic resolution, Tung further reinforces it with the dramatic episode of the slaying of the fish.

It may be argued that there is a contradiction here, and indeed there is. If the fish is subjective to Monkey, that is, a part of Monkey's mind,[26] how can it at the same time be treated objectively and be slain by Monkey? The contradiction is brought on by the fact that at this point the story and the theme meet. The externalization of the fish is necessary for the story, since the fish is treated in the scheme of the supplement as yet another monster seeking to devour the Monk. Thus, the fish in this function relates directly to Tripitaka and the other disciples. But at the same time, thematically the fish is explained as merely an aberration in

Monkey's mind. The contradiction comes in the clash between the narrative and conceptual materials, yet it is acceptable to the reader, and for the following important reason. The contradiction does not destroy the artistic effect of the conclusion, because it is finally resolved by the fact that it is Monkey who also destroys the illusion in his own mind. Thus the story and the theme which were in contradiction now converge and the contradiction is resolved.

The last episode in the conclusion provides the final stroke for unifying the whole theme of the novel. The line from the *Book of Changes* on which the teacher is lecturing reflects the same world-view as the opening poem in the novel. Cosmic reality is a unity which includes all. A proper understanding of this will dispel illusion and will not be in error. Tung thus ends his novel thematically at exactly the same place where he began it, and this provides a coherence which is highly satisfying to the reader.

## V   *Central Concepts in the Theme*

It now remains for us to isolate the three central concepts on which the theme is based. The first is the concept of *ch'ing,* which I am translating as "desire."

Although in Chinese today the word is used in several different ways,[27] its basic meaning is still what appears to have been its early one, namely, that of emotion or feeling. The *Li Chi (Book of Rites)* gives the following seven kinds of *ch'ing: hsi* (joy), *nu* (anger), *ai* (sorrow), *chü* (fear), *ai* (love), *wu* (hate), and *yü* (wish or desire).[28] The *Shuo-wen* (a Han dynasty etymological dictionary) defines the word as "the *yin force in man, that which harbors yü* (wish or desire)."[29]

Buddhism came to China in the Han dynasty, and the word *ch'ing* was used to express one of its central ideas, that of desire. Buddhist doctrine derives from the four Noble Truths conveyed by Gautama himself. These are that life is *dukkha* or suffering, that the cause of this suffering is *tanha* or desire, that suffering can be terminated by eliminating desire, and that the way to eliminate desire is to follow the Eightfold Path proclaimed by the Buddha.[30]

Desire comes about, according to the Buddhists, as a result of ignorance. There is therefore a close relationship between *ch'ing* as desire and *hsin* as mind. An individual desires and craves for that which is illusory and impermanent, because he suffers from ignorance as to the true nature of things. Fung Yu-lan has summarized this aspect of Buddhist doctrine as follows:

All things in the universe are the manifestations of the mind and therefore are illusory and impermanent, yet the individual ignorantly craves for and cleaves to them. This fundamental Ignorance is called *Avidya,* which in Chinese is translated as *Wu-ming,* nonenlightenment. From ignorance comes the craving for and cleaving to life, because of which the individual is bound to the eternal Wheel of Birth and Death, from which he can never escape.[31]

It is significant to note here that there is a tradition which associates desire as well as the mind with monkeys. The compound *ch'ing-yüan* (monkey of desire) occurs commonly in Chinese. A Buddhist dictionary explains it in this way: "One says 'the monkey of desire' because mental desires are changing and unsettled, just like monkeys."[32]

Another common compound in Chinese is *hsin-yüan* (monkey of the mind), which often appears together with *yi-ma* (horse of the will). Glen Dudbridge has made a study of these compounds as allegorical terms which have been incorporated into the *Hsi-yu chi.*[33] In reference to the monkey of the mind, he writes:

The metaphor makes its point simply and graphically: the random uncontrollable movements of the monkey symbolize the waywardness of the native human mind before it achieves a composure which only Buddhist discipline can effect.[34]

In supporting his theme with the story of a monkey with a wandering mind who is beguiled by a monster of desire, Tung was in harmony with a long tradition which came down through the *Hsi-yu chi.*

A second basic concept, which proceeds from the first, is that of *huan* (illusion). When the mind goes astray it does not understand the true nature of things. Ignorant of reality, it desires that which is impermanent and thus is surrounded by an unreal world. This is also distinctively Buddhist, and the word *huan* appears repeatedly in Buddhist texts. Extensive treatment is given to this concept in the *Yüan-chüeh ching (Sutra of Perfect Awareness).* This sutra was translated during the T'ang dynasty by the Buddhist monk Buddhatrata,[35] and its ideas are remarkably similar to what we find in the *His-yu pu.*

There is a tradition which associates this *sutra* with Tung Yüeh. It is said that as a child he requested that he begin his studies with this text, and possibly this was one of his favorite books.[36]

The *sutra* contains the record of conversations between the Buddha and some of his disciples. At one point the Buddha says:

Good sons, it is the case with all those living things that since the body of illusion is destroyed, therefore the mind of illusion is also destroyed. Since the mind of illusion is destroyed, therefore the world of illusion is also destroyed. Since the world of illusion is destroyed, therefore the destruction of illusion is also destroyed. Since the destruction of illusion is destroyed, therefore nothing has been destroyed that is not illusion. To give an example, when you polish all the dirt from a mirror, its brightness appears.[37]

Frequently in the text the Buddha recites *gathas* to his disciples. He begins one of them by saying:

> P'u-hsien, you should know
> That all living things
> Have no beginning, and are illusory and
> without enlightenment.[38]

He begins another in this way:

> P'u-yen, you should know
> That in the case of all living things
> The mind of the body is as an illusion.[39]

Here living things first and then specifically the mind of the body are identified with illusion. This is similar to something said by Tripitaka in the *Hsi-yu chi*. He leaves Ch'ang-an and after several days on the road visits with the Monks of the Fa-men Szu (Monastery of the Gate of the Law). These monks talk of the many dangers ahead on the Westward Journey and at first Tripitaka is silent. Then he simply points to his mind and says:[40]

When the mind becomes alive, then the many kinds of demons become alive. When the mind is extinguished, then the many kinds of demons are extinguished.[41]

Thus the central concept of the *Hsi-yu pu,* that demons are products of the mind and therefore illusory, is found in the earlier novel. In his novel, Tung frequently raises the question of the real versus the unreal, the true versus the false. This is part of Monkey's continual perplexity in the dream. Are the places he visits and the characters he meets real or not?

Not only is Monkey involved with the question of illusion through that which comes into his experience, but he also contributes to the whole illusory effect by continually refusing to act as himself. In his dream Monkey usually participates indirectly.[42] In the New T'ang he is an observer. In the World of the Ancients he is in disguise. In the World of the Future he serves as a substitute for the King of Hell, Yen-lo (Yama). In the Green, Green World proper, he is again in disguise most of the time, first by hiding his true identity from the old Taoist and then by acting as his own double, Six-Eared Monkey, when joining the army. The total effect of this is to bolster the sense of illusion, for Monkey seldom is, as it were, really himself.

A third central concept proceeds from the first two, and that is *wu* (enlightenment). In Buddhist thought enlightenment comes when the mind ceases to be attached by desire to the transient, phenomenal world. Freed from attachment, it no longer claims a separate identity and may fuse with the universal, all-encompassing mind of the Buddha. Just as illusion is generated by the mind, so also enlightenment may be achieved by the mind. Since illusion is self-induced, enlightenment must be self-realized.

This emphasis on the self is brought out clearly in two places. There is, first, Monkey's experience in the Ke-lei Kung (Palace of Vines and Creepers) in Chapter 10. Monkey has now returned to the Green, Green World proper and finds himself once again in the Tower of Myriad Mirrors. When he tries to get out through the balustrades, however, he is caught by them and immobilized until an old man comes along who frees him.

> Monkey then got free, expressed his thanks, and asked, "Venerable Old Man, what is your name? When I see the Buddha I want to record great merit on your behalf." The old man, said, "Great Sage, I am called Sun Wu-k'ung." Monkey said, "I too am called Sun Wu-k'ung."[43]

Monkey inquires further into the old man's history, only to find that the old man claims, in fact, to be Monkey himself. Angered by this apparent imposter, Monkey pulls out his cudgel to fight.

The old man shook his sleeves[44] and walked off, calling out, "This is just what is called a person saving himself. Too bad you take what is not true as true and what is true as not true."[45] Suddenly a ray of golden light shot into [Monkey's] eyes and then the form of the old man was not to be seen. Monkey then realized that it was his own true spirit that had appeared, and so quickly he again said a word of thanks, to thank himself.[46]

Although this is but one episode in the dream, it carries the concept of self-enlightenment or self-salvation, which is basic to the whole novel, as exemplified by the explicit reference by the old man to what is true and what is not true.

A second passage in which self-enlightenment is stressed is found in the last chapter. The Master of the Void awakens Monkey from his dream, explains about the Mackerel and his background, and then recites a *gatha*, which will be quoted in full because of its importance.

> And there were no spring-time boys and girls,
>    For these were the roots of the Mackerel;
> And there was no new Son of Heaven,
>    For this was the power of the Mackerel;
> And there was no green bamboo broom,
>    For this was the name of the Mackerel;
> And there was no general's commission,
>    For this was the writing of the Mackerel;
> And there were no axes hacking at the sky,
>    For these were the shapes of the Mackerel;
> And there was no Prince Little Moon,
>    For this was the spirit of the Mackerel;
> And there was no Myriad Mirror Tower,
>    For this was the accomplishment of the Mackerel;
> And there were no people in the mirrors,
>    For these were the bodies of the Mackerel;
> And there was no World of Headaches,[47]
>    For this was the inspiration of the Mackerel;
> And there was no Lü-chu Lou (Green Pearl Tower),[48]
>    For this was the mind of the Mackerel;
> And there was no Hsiang Yü of Ch'u,
>    For this was the soul of the Mackerel;
> And there was no Beauty Yü,
>    For this was the delerium of the Mackerel;
> And there was no King Yen-lo,
>    For this was the realm of the Mackerel;

And there was no World of the Ancients,
   For this was the accomplishment of the Mackerel;
And there was no World of the Future,
   For this was the crystallization of the Mackerel;
And there were no *chieh* hexagram accounts,
   For this was the palace of the Mackerel;
And there was no T'ang chief minister,
   For this was the creation of the Mackerel;
And there were no songs and dances,
   For these were the nature of the Mackerel;
And there was no crying of Maid Kingfisher,
   For this was the fulfillment of the Mackerel;
And there was no platform for roll call of the troops,
   For this was the activity of the Mackerel;
And there was no battle with Prince Paramita,
   For this was the din of the Mackerel;
And there was no Mackerel,
   For this was Monkey's desire.[49]

In the above *gatha,* the first twenty-one couplets all follow the same pattern. In the first half one element in Monkey's dream is isolated and said to be nonexistent. In the second half its nonexistence is explained by identifying it with some part or aspect of the Mackerel or his activity. The real point of the poem is its summation, which comes in the last couplet. The Mackerel himself is said to be nonexistent for he is, in fact, Monkey's desire. Thus, the whole dream is seen as Monkey's self-delusion. Immediately following the *gatha* comes the episode in which Monkey returns to his Master the Monk, and recognizing the Mackerel in the disguise of a new disciple, he slays it. He has experienced enlightenment.

Thus, we have in the three central concepts of the novel a full statement of the basic Buddhist understanding of life. The progression is from desire to illusion and from illusion to enlightenment. The theme as a Buddhist fable is complete.

CHAPTER 7

# Hsi-yu pu *World as Dream (Psychological Realism)*

IN the foregoing three chapters I have approached the *Hsi-yu pu* analytically. Its verbal, narrative, and conceptual materials have been identified and discussed, and it has been shown how these make up the language, the story, and the theme of the novel. Now it is necessary to take a different approach and to move from analysis to synthesis.

Here I adopt the concept of an overall structure which brings unity to the various materials. The word I use for this is "world." The distinction between materials and world is not that of the old dichotomy between form and content. Indeed, it will be observed that the three kinds of materials considered contain elements of both form and content. Rather the distinction is now made along aesthetic lines. The world is that which makes the novel aesthetically effective. It is that which brings the various materials together to form a coherent and comprehensive whole. It is that which reveals the overall purpose or meaning behind the novel.

When considering the novel's world in this way we are immediately confronted by the problem of its complexity, and this arises in at least two separate ways. First, as a supplement, it shares the complexity of the *Hsi-yu chi*. That this former novel contains a highly complex world of its own can easily be demonstrated by the many ways in which it has been interpreted. Mainland Chinese critics see in it political satire.[1] Traditional critics have stressed its religious allegory.[2] One missionary even saw it as a Buddho-Christian novel.[3] C. T. Hsia emphasizes the comedy and myth found in it.[4] As a genuine supplement, the *Hsi-yu pu* inherits part of this complexity.

Yet, because of the prominence of the dream in the novel, its world is distinctive, and the complexity of this world arises largely from the fact that it must be defined in terms of various levels of meaning connected with the dream. Not only are elements in the dream themselves symbolic, but the dream as a whole lends itself to several interpretations.

In this and the following chapters I shall examine this complex world of the *Hsi-yu pu*. It will be presented at three levels: as dream, as satire, and as myth. In this chapter, I begin with the world as dream. Here the novel is seen as a study in psychological realism, and this term is used because at this level the novel becomes simply a realistic portrayal of dreams. Insofar as it deals with dreams it is psychological, and insofar as its focus is on the dream itself, together with its causes, its internal workings, and its outcome, it is realistic. The world here is that of the dreamer as a dreamer. That is to say, the focus is on the dreamer and his dream, now not seen symbolically but rather for what they are in themselves.

## I  *Tung Yüeh and Dreams*

We know that in his life Tung Yüeh was greatly interested in dreams. He himself often had dreams and apparently took more than just a passing interest in them. Also, he wrote about dreams, for in addition to his novel we find in his collections of poetry frequent references to dreams. Most important of all, however, are four prose selections on dreams found in his *Feng-ts'ao An ch'ien-chi (Former Collection from the Abundant Grass Hermitage)*. These appear in succession with his writings listed for the year 1643, which is two years after the date when the novel appears to have first been published. The four selections are:

1. "Chao-yang meng shih hsü" (Preface to a History of Dreams of Chao-yang).
2. "Meng-hsiang chih" (Monograph on Dream Lands).
3. "Cheng-meng p'ien" (On Testing Dreams).
4. "Meng She yüeh" (Dream Society Contract).

In studying the materials in these essays, three things of significance stand out. The first is that for Tung Yüeh dreams are like being drunk with wine. What one sees and experiences is illusory and is comparable to what one sees when watching clouds take various forms and shapes in the sky.

In the "Preface to a History of Dreams of Chao-yang," Tung first tells us of a dream:

I climbed the K'un-lun Shan (K'un-lun Mountain) and observed the palaces of the gods and immortals. I feasted on the flowers of a hundred plants and fanned myself with the tail-feathers of a white phoenix. Not until after the cock crowed and the sun arose did I know it was a dream.[5]

He then uses the metaphor of the cloud to describe the dream. When clouds touch the rocks and then rise and move about in the sky they appear to be dragons, lions, flying horses, etc. Here a string of thirty-one images is given which include not only animals, people, and ghosts, but also colors, objects of nature, buildings, etc. Tung then concludes:

Therefore, as floating clouds change and transform, the heavenly patterns are constantly new. And as one soars in dreams, the spirit is not destroyed. Thus, clouds are like being mad and dreams are like being drunk. The ancients were fond of being drunk and even praised the virtue of drunkenness. Gentlemen of later times will see (i.e., understand) from this why I cherish dreams.[6]

But dreams are more than simply being in a state of drunken euphoria. They actually introduce us into a world of their own and this leads to a second point about these passages. In the "Monograph on Dream Lands," Tung describes these lands. There are seven of them and they are like the Chung-kuo Chiu-chou (Nine Provinces of China).[7] Tung writes:

The first is called "Hsüan-kuai Hsiang" (Land of the Dark and the Strange), an in this land birds wear hats and beasts were belts. The grasses fly and trees walk. And there are humanlike horns and fishlike bodies.[8]
The second is called "Shan-shui Hsiang" (Land of Mountains and Rivers), and here there are loftly mountains and great rivers.
The third is called "Ming Hsiang" (Land of Darkness), and this is the land where all the ghosts wandering [Mount] Tai are.[9]
The fourth is called "Shih Hsiang" (Land of Consciousness). In it are fortifications of desire and ramparts of mental activity fabricated by concentrated thought.
The fifth is called "Ju-yi Hsiang" (Land of As-you-wish). Here there are high terraces and winding houses; gold, jade, and precious pearls; the five colors and kingfisher blue; strange birds and unusual beasts; beautiful

women; bells and drums, caps and garments; poems and books not yet burned;[10] and rare amusements and secret meetings. Everyone has what he wants.

The sixth is called "Ts'ang-wang Hsiang" (Land of the Hidden Past), and all former affairs belong here.

The seventh is called "Wei-lai Hsiang" (Land of the Future). Here it is possible by knowing the future to cause people not to worry over wandering sons far away.[11]

It will be noted that these lands of dreams involve a dimension of experience which goes beyond the limits of the dreamer's own subjective mind. This is a dimension of reality which exceeds the individual and his own past. It transcends the boundaries of time and space. It includes not only wishes, thought, and fantasy, but also nature and the world of the spirits, as well as the past and the future.

Finally, Tung believed that in dreams there is a balancing out of opposite extremes. Conscious life may reflect one thing and a dream its opposite. There is the following remarkable section in the "Dream Society Contract:"

The way of dreams seems to be like the *Yi* [-*ching*] (*Book of Changes*). Dreams are what the rich and honored, those with great leisure and happiness, and those who are peaceful do not want, but are what the poor and lowly, the sorrowful, and those in a disorderly world make offerings for and seek after. If rich and honored people dream of poverty and lowliness, they will lose their riches and honor. People with great leisure and happiness will become destitute of these things if they dream of sorrow. People who are peaceful will find themselves in a world of disorder if they dream of disorder. And so, when poor and degraded, one ought to dream; when sorrowful, one ought to dream; and when in a world of disorder, one ought to dream.[12]

Tung bases his understanding of dreams on ancient Taoist philosophy. There is a dualism of extremes forever reaching for a balance, and the medium of compensation for an extreme is a dream. This concept bears striking similarity to the modern notion of the subconscious appearing in a dream to release that which has been repressed by the conscious.

It is not surprising to find that Tung's views on dreams are reflected in his novel. While the novel may have been written several years before these essays, still the basic viewpoint in both appears to be the same.

Tung regarded dreams as illusory. He compared them with drunkenness and with clouds which shift and change their forms. In the novel, the dream is a prolonged experience of illusion. What Monkey experiences in his dream is not real, for it is all the result of his own mind, which has gone astray through the deceptive power of desire. The Buddhist theme promotes the idea that dreams are illusory. This does not mean, of course, that dreams stand in contrast with wakeful life, which is "real." To the Buddhist, all of life as an unenlightened man experiences it is illusory. Rather, the dream heightens the effect of the general illusion.

The seven different kinds of dreamlands suggested by Tung also appear in the novel. There is the dark and strange as represented by Prince Little Moon and his Green, Green World, with the Tower of Myriad Mirrors and its balustrades that change shape and have the power to engangle and ensnare the unwary. There is nature, with all its beauty and majesty which is first seen in the scene with the peonies and later in Monkey's trip to the Green Bamboo Cave. There are the ghosts and spirits of the underworld in Monkey's experience in hell. There is the emphasis on the power of the mind in the allegory on desire. There is the enjoyment of sensual pleasures in Monkey's experiences with the beautiful ladies and the Monk's entertainment in the Green, Green World. There are characters and events brought in from the past, as in the World of the Ancients, and there is also the projection in time of the World of the Future.

Finally, underlying the entire dream is the principle of duality, with its pull toward a balance between two opposites. Monkey continually experiences this, because his security becomes insecurity, his faith, as for instance in the monk, is shattered, and his normal strength is of no avail to him.

At the level of psychological realism, Tung was operating within his own understanding of what dreams represent. Interesting as it may be to point out the extent to which his understanding equates with our own, yet we must be careful not to confuse the two, for this can only impair our appreciation of the novel. At the level of world as dream, Tung presents us with a fictional dreamer, but this he does on his own terms.

## II  *An Early Interpretation*

The first attempt at interpretation of the novel in reference to a given position on dreams comes in Layman Yi-ju's preface. Here we read:

> In supplementing the *Westward Journey,* wherein shall we say the significance lies? After the three provocations for the palm leaf fan, when the flames had been extinguished and the fire cooled, the author by metaphor spoke important words. Being aware that the demons of desire were gathering and that their forms were appearing without limit, he followed the confusion of a realm of dreams and on a pillow conjured up a whole great world.
>
> Thus, the fact that Monkey Sun beat to death a group of boys and girls under the peonie flowers, that following spring colts in a prairie fire he suddenly entered the New T'ang, that he heard about the Li Shan T'u (Picture of Mount Li) and then thought of borrowing the Ch'ü-shan To (Bell for Driving off Mountains), makes it seem that the shadow of the palm leaf fan had not yet dispersed. This was a *szu-meng* (dream of thought).
>
> As soon as he fell into the Green, Green World he necessarily reached the myriad mirrors and was completely confused. The walking in space and the hacking at the sky were all produced by fear of the thought that Ch'en Hsüan-tsang was serving as the Great General, Slayer of the Green.[13] This was an *e-meng* (dream of alarm).
>
> He wanted to see Ch'in Shin-huang (First Emperor of Ch'in) but suddenly bumped into [Hsiang Yü, King of] Hsi Ch'u (West Ch'u). At first he entered the Ku-jen Ching (Mirror of the Ancients). He searched, but then again it was the future. In the case in which Ch'in Kuei, the Prime Minister of Sung, was cross-examined, punishment was very severe,[14] and this dispelled the uncommon resentment of several hundred years in history. This was close to a *cheng-meng* (normal dream).
>
> He got into trouble in the Palace of Vines and Brambles and then was released near Ch'ou Feng-ting (Sorrow Peak). The drama was performed and the ballad played and all that he observed and experienced was of greatest danger and most frustrating. It was that which is called "vast billows and white waves." When it was just right for him to exert his strength, there was no place for him to exert his strength. This was a *chü-meng* (dream of fear).
>
> Among the roots of desire of all times the one most difficult to destroy is [that designated by] the word *se* (sex). When Beauty Yü Hsi Shih, Szu Szu, Green Pearl, Maid Kingfisher Cord, and Duckweed Fragrance teased and joked in the women's quarters, their beauty and charm came near to people and their romantic words soared high. Naturally this called forth [Monkey's] basic sexuality. It seems that this was near to a *hsi-meng* (dream of joy).
>
> When it came to Prince Paramita's recognition of Monkey as his father, the stars were few and the moon was bright and the great dream was about

to end. When the colors of the five flags were in confusion, he was about to come out of the demonic, and this could be a *wu-meng* (dream of waking).[15]

Here Layman Yi-ju is applying a scheme for classifying dreams to Monkey's dream. the scheme is found in the ancient classic, the *Chou Li (Rites of Chou)*, which states:

As for interpreters of dreams, they shall manage the times and seasons and shall observe [the times when the signs of] Heaven and earth meet. They shall distinguish the vital forces of the *yin* and the *yang*. Then from the sun, moon, stars, and planets they shall interpret the good and evil of the six dreams. The first of these is called a *cheng-meng* (normal dream). The second is called an *e-meng* (dream of alarm). The third is called a *szu-meng* (dream of thought). The fourth is called a *wu-meng* (dream of waking). The fifth is called a *hsi-meng* (dream of joy). And the sixth is called a *chü-meng* (dream of fear).[16]

Extensive commentary for this classic was provided by Cheng Hsüan.[17] Regarding this classification, Cheng explained that a normal dream is a spontaneous, peaceful dream occurring without stimulation. A dream of alarm occurs when one is startled by something. A dream of thought occurs when one thinks about something when awake and then dreams about it. A dream of waking occurs when one speaks of something when awake and then dreams of it. A dream of joy occurs when one is happy. A dream of fear occurs when one is frightened.[18]

This classification became a part of Chinese tradition. It was taken up by the writer of the *Lieh-tzu,* who incorporated it into his discussion of the meaning of wakefulness and dreams. In A. C. Graham's translation, the relevant passage reads:

There are eight proofs of being awake, six tests of dreaming. What is meant by the eight proofs? They are events and actions, gain and loss, sorrow and joy, birth and death. These eight happen when the body encounters something. What is meant by the six tests? There are normal dreams, and dreams due to alarm, thinking, memory, rejoicing, fear. These six happen when the spirit connects with something. Those who do not recognize where the changes excited in them come from are perplexed about the reasons when an event arrives. Those who do recognize where they come from do know the reason; and if you know the reason nothing will startle you.[19]

In analyzing this traditional classification, two things are signifi-

cant. The first is that dreams are seen to stand in a causal relationship with wakeful experiences. The exception is in the case of normal dreams, which Cheng Hsüan takes as occurring spontaneously.
In all other cases, however, the dreamer has an experience, often
emotional, which is reflected in his dream. The writer of the *Lieh-
tzu* expands this by suggesting that dreams occur when the spirit
connects with something which is part of the larger objective world
external to the dreamer.

This leads to the idea that since dreams reflect external reality
they may be usefully interpreted. And so we have from the earliest
times the function of prognostication connected with dreams. As
the *Rites of Chou* indicates, officials were appointed as interpreters
of dreams. The dreams were not seen in isolation, but rather as
reflections of a larger interrelated reality. The dream interpreters
were to arrive at their conclusions not only on the basis of the
dream itself, but also in relation to astronomical signs, calendric
calculations, and natural phenomena.

In adopting the classification system of the *Rites of Chou,*
Layman Yi-ju accepts the idea that dreams reflect wakeful experiences and may be interpreted in light of them. When he speaks of
the demons of desire gathering and their forms appearing, he is
speaking of Monkey's experiences prior to the supplement and
more especially of those connected with Madam Raksasa. He sees
the dream as a composite one containing within itself all of the six
kinds in the classification. At one point he differs from Cheng
Hsüan and the writer of the *Lieh Tzu*. He takes a dream of waking
not to mean one which reflects something spoken while awake or
something remembered, but rather one which occurs just prior to
the waking experience. Significantly, he puts the trial of Ch'in Kuei
and his punishment in the category of the normal dream and even
refers to the "uncommon resentment of several hundred years."
Thus, he does not see this episode as resulting from an unusual
experience of Monkey's, but rather as that which might occur
naturally.

Layman Yi-ju takes the dream as a composite dream and therefore sees it reflecting differing aspects of Monkey's experiences: it
reflects his characteristic thought processes; his alarms, especially
those occasioned by his doubts about Tripitaka; his fears; and
finally his vulnerability to female attractions.

It is not possible to know to what extent Layman Yi-ju's views
coincided with Tung Yüeh's own. We may assume, however, that

they were similar. After all, the two were presumably friends, lived at the same time, and shared the same intellectual and cultural tradition. Furthermore, the preface appeared in Tung's own 1641 edition of the novel, and it is hardly likely that he would have included it had he not shared its basic views. As for the classification scheme of the *Rites of Chou,* Tung accepted its validity and referred to it in his own writings. For instance, in his "Dream Society Contract" he cites the classic and lists the six kinds of dreams.[20] It is not unreasonable to assume that in Layman Yi-ju's preface we see reflected Tung's own intention insofar as he wished his novel to be taken as a realistic study of dreams.

### III    *Modern Interpretations*

Two modern scholars, T. A. Hsia and Robert E. Hegel, have interpreted the *Hsi-yu pu* primarily at the level of its world as dream. T. A. Hsia in "The *Hsi Yu Pu* as a Study of Dreams in Fiction" sees the distinctiveness of Tung's novel precisely within the context of psychological realism. Speaking of Tung, he says:

But he distinguished himself by not being an imitator. He did not simply invent another episode to extend a pilgrimage which, in the original, was anything but short. In his book the pilgrimage is used for a new purpose. It is used as a framework to present certain truths about dreams. Since such truths are rarely touched upon in Chinese literature, Tung Yüeh's conscious reworking of the myth of the Pilgrimage may be said to be a unique contribution.[21]

According to Hsia, Tung's purpose is realized through the demands of the narrative. The Mackerel is presented as the most formidable adversary Monkey has encountered, with its immense power and great potential for exerting evil influence. Such a monster obviously required special treatment.

To do full justice to Monkey's temptation by, and struggle with, the Ch'ing Fish Spirit requires a narrative method which Tung Yüeh has to devise for himself. There is little he can borrow from Wu Ch'eng-en. His method is the creation of dreams, dreams with features familiar to dreamers all over the world: distortions, discrepancies, inconsequence, irrelevance, and preposterous happenings imbued with emotional tensions.[22]

The whole dream sequence is characterized by a sense of bafflement which leads to anxiety. Monkey is at first baffled by the New T'ang and its inconsistency with reality as he knows it. Soon bafflement gives way to anxiety, which becomes increasingly intense as the dream progresses. Hsia takes the anxiety as a reflection of the various reasons Monkey has for feeling insecure.

Monkey has a number of reasons to feel insecure: the journey yet to be accomplished with all its dreaded difficulties, his duty to protect his defenseless but gullible master Tripitaka, the tension in the master-disciple relationship caused by past misunderstandings, especially by the unjust punishments he has received at the hands of Tripitaka, and his suspicion of the purity of Tripitaka's motives, though after their experience in the Women's Kingdom, it should not seem likely that the holy man will give up his monastic vows and marry or take a mistress. His close association with Tripitaka may also have awakened his Buddhist conscience, so that he perhaps feels his hands stained with the blood of many lives and his effort to humanize himself a failure.[23]

The relationship between Monkey's anxiety and the Flaming Mountain episode is also stressed. Through its portrayal of romantic involvement with Madam Raksasa, this episode reveals a weakness in Monkey and thus he shows himself susceptible to the fish's temptations. This is reflected most clearly when Monkey hears reference made to his five sons and in the end faces one of them in battle.

Although Hsia emphasizes what I call psychological realism, he is careful to show that the novel must be understood for its general psychological validity and not as an attempt to produce an actual dream.[24] Both Hsia and Layman Yi-ju see Monkey's dream as reflecting his wakeful experiences. Also, both interpret the dream in a composite framework: Layman Yi-ju uses the classification scheme in the *Rites of Chou* and Hsia a general modern view of human psychology.

In Robert Hegel's study we have an attempt to interpret Monkey's dream in terms of a single modern theory of dreams, that of Freudian psychoanalysis. Hegel takes the theory expounded in Freud's classic work, *The Interpretation of Dreams,* and applies this directly to Tung's novel. Freud believed that all dreams involve a process of desired wish fulfillment. That is to say, the dreamer has certain wishes which for one reason or another are not fulfilled in his conscious life. These are suppressed into the subconscious.

During sleep the conscious relaxes its control, with the result that the repressed wishes come to the surface and appear in hallucinatory form as dreams. Their appearance is invariably symbolic; therefore, much of the success in dream interpretation will depend on the skill with which symbols are identified and understood. Also, since the conscious never disappears totally even in the deepest dream, often a conflict situation is set up in which repressed wishes seek fulfillment but are prevented from being so by the continued activity of the conscious.

Hegel takes from Freudian theory three possible wishes which may serve as instigators in Monkey's dream. The first is the wish associated with the sex drive. Evidence of latent sexuality in Monkey is seen in the Madam Raksasa temptation, and also in the experience of seeing the women and children by the peonies. Although Monkey slaughters the women and children, Hegel says, "One may logically assume that these women favorably impressed our Great Sage."[25]

Dream symbolism is also seen as revealing Monkey's sexuality. Hegel lists pertinent Freudian sex symbols as follows:

Staircases and the like represent the sex act; landscapes with wooded hills may describe the genitals symbolically. Beating a child and decapitation may be portrayed in dreams to symbolize masturbation and castration respectively.... A house may symbolize the human body; a pavilion might indicate a place for sexual intercourse.[26]

With these Freudian symbols at hand, it is an easy matter to find corresponding elements in the novel. Although there are no staircases to be found, as Hegel points out, there is a Tower of Myriad Mirrors without a staircase, and perhaps this is significant.[27] Also, there are descriptions of landscapes. At the beginning of the novel children are beaten,[28] and at the end of the dream Tripitaka is beheaded. Then there are the many, many palaces in Chapter 11, and it does not require much effort to imagine what a Freudian interpretation will do with these.

A second possible dream instigator is Monkey's desire for freedom from his obligations to Tripitaka. As Hegel explains:

Throughout *Hsi-yu chi* Monkey had resented figures of authority and had longed to be truly free. But then he became bound to this muddle-headed old monk, both by vows and by the spell that activates the metal "conscience'' around Monkey's head. These restrictions provided effective censorship to his wish during waking life. Not so in dreams, however; while asleep Monkey's ego is free to smart from his master's freely-applied rebukes and to nourish his old desire for freedom. Thus it can hardly be disputed that a conflict raged within his mind, for he does feel genuine concern for Tripitaka's safety.[29]

Hegel traces this conflict throughout the whole dream, which now becomes a series of increasingly intense experiences in which first the subconscious and then the conscious dominates. The subconscious tries to keep Monkey away from Tripitaka, whereas the conscious tries to make Monkey assume his responsibilities and return to his master. Monkey's anguish is caused by the fact that both conflicting wishes, the subconscious and the conscious, are of nearly the same strength. The climax comes when the freedom wish finally succeeds in achieving its ultimate goal and Tripitaka is killed. At this point Monkey wakes up.

There is yet a third possible dream instigator, and this is Monkey's desire for punishment. Here the reasoning is that Monkey's wish for freedom leaves him with a feeling of guilt. This in turn generates a desire for punishment which becomes another wish working itself out. Hegel writes:

Thus one can see the kinds of punishment Monkey inflicts upon himself in his dream: isolation, defamation, embarrassment, helplessness, loss of self-confidence, repeated betrayal, physical tortures, the ultimate of grief and confusion. Monkey certainly paid dearly for this one indiscreet wish for freedom![30]

According to this theory, the most dramatic example of a desire for punishment is seen in the episode involving Ch'in Kuei. Here Hegel has Monkey identifying himself with Ch'in Kuei rather than with Yen-lo, this in spite of the fact that on the surface of things Monkey is taking the place of Yen-lo. Thus, Monkey sees himself as a traitor and, in punishing the traitor of the Sung, is in fact punishing himself.

Although Hegel suggests three possible dream instigators and in his study actually develops all three, he does not give them all equal weight. He writes:

In sum, Freudian analysis reveals that Monkey's dream embodies at least one of two possible repressed wishes, either for freedom from bondage to Tripitaka or to punish himself for his past shortcomings. A third possible dream-instigator exists, a repressed sexual urge, but this interpretation is less consistent with Monkey's personality than are the others. His dream consists of numerous symbols and symbolic situations which lend themselves well to either of the two more logical interpretations.[31]

Hegel believes that Freudian theory can well be applied to Monkey's dream. Since it is taken as inspired by Tung's own dreams, it is seen to reflect a universal human phenomenon. Hegel's enthusiasm for the Freudian interpretation is best expressed by his own words:

Indeed, reading *Hsi-yu pu* in conjunction with Freud's *The Interpretation of Dreams* gives one the disquieting impression that Tung read the latter before writing his novel. Since Tung also carried on research into his own dreams, it seems reasonable to conclude that he must have discovered many of the same truths about dreams as did Freud.[32]

These are confident words and they serve well to conclude a most significant and carefully developed study. Hegel's considerable contribution lies in the fact that he has been able to take one Western theory and show how the novel may be interpreted by it.

There are, however, three problems connected with an orthodox Freudian approach. The first concerns the problem of the composite approach versus the single-theme approach to the dream. I have already shown how both Layman Yi-ju and T. A. Hsia take the composite approach. That is to say, they see several possible themes all brought together in one fictional dream. Freud believed that all dreams "fulfill a wish on the part of the dreamer."[33] He also believed that "all dreams which occur on the same night are only variations on a single theme."[34] Hegel adopts this Freudian view and therefore is bound not only to interpret the dream exclusively as wish fulfillment, but having isolated three possible wishes, he also finds it necessary to push for a choice for only one of these as the possible dream theme.

There are two things which argue against this narrow Freudian view. The first is that the dream in the novel is a fictional dream. Even if the Freudian view were valid, there is no reason why, as a fictional dream, it should not be taken as a composite one. Secondly, the Freudian analysis is largely out of date, and the view that any given dream is always the expression of one wish-fulfillment theme is an oversimplification. Carl Jung may serve as a convenient representative of the reaction against Freud. Jung wrote:

> The view that dreams are merely imaginary fulfillments of suppressed wishes has long ago been superseded. It is certainly true that there are dreams which embody suppressed wishes and fears, but what is there which the dream cannot on occasion embody? Dreams may give expression to ineluctable truths, to philosophical pronouncements, illusions, wild fantasies, memories, plans, anticipations, irrational experiences, even telepathic visions, and heaven knows what besides.[35]

A second problem concerns the uncritical equation of *ch'ing* with Freudian wish themes. Hegel has done us all a great service in pointing out the importance and place of *ch'ing* in the novel. Yet, it is misleading simply to identify this Chinese concept with the Freudian wish. We must remember that the dream was consciously produced by Tung Yüeh. Therefore, his views are important in any attempt to understand it. The obvious point here is that there was a great difference between Tung and Freud. The two came out of vastly different cultures and widely differing traditions. Freud lived and worked in Vienna among members of the bourgeois middle class. Tung lived and worked among disillusioned intellectuals in seventeenth-century China. Freud operated out of the Judeo-Christian tradition dominated by a theism with its related syndrome of sin, guilt, and punishment. Tung was in a cultural tradition where Buddhist, Taoist, and Confucian values were dominant. Of the three wish themes Hegel identifies in the novel, probably the first one concerning sex is most easily interpreted as *ch'ing,* yet this is the very one Hegel himself finally rejects. Both the freedom wish and the punishment wish present difficulties. As understood within the Buddhist context, *ch'ing* is essentially desire for attachment both intellectually and emotionally to the transient things of this world. Thus, the concept of freedom as applied to the dream is best thought of not as movement away from the Monk but as movement toward the Monk. Monkey has shown himself susceptible just because he has revealed in the Flaming Mountain episode that he is not free of *ch'ing,* or attachment to the temporal world. In the light of the novel's Buddhist theme, Monkey's real freedom comes when he is enlightened and returns to the Monk. Hegel's Freudian view is understandable, yet it distorts, for it shifts the emphasis away from the Buddhist idea of *ch'ing* as attachment and, in fact, gives it the opposite connotation.

A third problem is raised by Hegel's identification of *ch'ing* with the punishment wish. Involved here is a broader problem inherent in the whole of Freudian psychology. This is that Freudian theory bases its psychological formulations on the sick rather than on the healthy mind. Jung writes:

Freud's teaching is definitely one-sided in that it generalizes from facts that are relevant only to neurotic states of mind; its validity is really confined to those states.[36]

This limitation is reflected in Hegel's analysis. To interpret the punishment of Ch'in Kuei as, in fact, the expression of Monkey's subconscious desire to punish himself assumes nothing less than a sick, neurotic Monkey. Our Great Sage would have to be filled with a morbid sense of guilt to wish for the horrible kinds of punishment inflicted on Ch'in Kuei in Chapter 9. It is difficult to believe that Tung intended to portray such a Monkey. As I shall show in the next chapter, this episode is best interpreted as belonging to another level of the novel's world.

# CHAPTER 8

# Hsi-yu pu *World as Satire (Social Protest)*

I N the previous chapter the world of the *Hsi-yu pu* was seen as that of dream. This is the most obvious level, since it takes the novel precisely for what it is on the surface: the story of a fictional monkey who has a dream. However, it is also the narrowest level, for it limits the world to the fictional context of the Westward Journey and its relevance for the reader to truths about dreams conveyed through this context.

To see the novel only at this first level is to view it, as it were, wearing blinders, for indeed the author's purpose extends beyond his desire merely to tell us something about dreams. His purpose may be socially as well as psychologically defined. Indirectly, through the use of the dream in the novel, Tung Yüeh is saying important things about his society. Inasmuch as the form of his social commentary is both critical and provocative of amusement and contempt, we may identify it as satirical.

Satire has been defined as "the literary art of diminishing a subject by making it ridiculous and evoking toward it attitudes of amusement, contempt, indignation, or scorn."[1] Thus, it differs from comedy, which seeks to evoke laughter for its own sake. Satire flourishes in the *Hsi-yu pu,* and there are at least two important reasons for this: the Buddhist theme provides the necessary standard or ideal against which satire is projected and the use of dream provides a suitable vehicle for the kind of distortion necessary in satire.[2]

In the West satire has a history which goes as far back as classical times,[3] and through the years well-defined forms have emerged.[4] It is clear that Chinese literature also has its satire, and this shows itself early in both poetry and works of prose.[5] A great deal more study is needed, however, before we shall be able to determine precisely the specific forms it takes in the Chinese tradition, or to understand how this tradition has developed. As for vernacular fiction, satire is surely best known through the eighteenth-century masterpiece *Ju-lin wai-shih* by Wu Ching-tzu.[6]

## I  *Objects of Satire*

There is a great deal of satire in the novel, and although much of it is of an incidental nature, five elements in Chinese life may be singled out as major objects of attack. These are given roughly in the order in which they are presented in the work itself.

### A.  *The imperial court*

Here the focus is on the emperor and the life he leads. The emperor is shown to be foolish and the life he leads transitory and meaningless. The agent used is a sweeping maid who appears to Monkey in Chapter 2. Early in his dream Monkey comes upon a strange place called the New T'ang, and after an unsuccessful attempt to determine if it is real or not, he bravely enters it. Soon afterwards he overhears a sweeping maid talking to herself and the information she supplies becomes Tung's satirical attack on imperial life in China.

In the first part of her speech the maid describes the ridiculous emperor with his ladies:

Ha! Ha! The emperor is asleep and the chief ministers are also asleep. The Green Jade Hall has now become a pavilion of sleeping immortals. Our romantic Son of Heaven spent last night with Lady Overthrower of States. They feasted in the Emerald Palace of the rear garden,[7] and drank heartily for the whole night. At first he [the emperor] pulled out a Kao-t'ang mirror,[8] told Lady Overthrower of States to stand on the left and Lady Hsü on the right,[9] and so the three of them stood there next to each other in front of the mirror. The Son of Heaven said, "[You] two ladies are beautiful," and Lady Overthrower of States said, "Your Majesty is beautiful." The Son of Heaven then turned his head around and asked us palace servants about this. Three or four hundred palace maids now answered with one voice,[10] "Indeed, an outstandingly [handsome] man." The Son of Heaven was greatly pleased and with a dazed look in his eyes drank a great cupful [of wine].

When he was half drunk with wine he got up and looked at the moon. The Son of Heaven then opened his mouth and laughed. Pointing to Ch'ang-e in the moon,[11] he said, "This is my Lady Hsü."

Lady Hsü then pointed to the Weaving Maid and the Cowherd and said,[12] "Here are Your Majesty and Lady Overthrower of States. Although tonight is the fifth day of the third moon, let us anticipate the celebration of the Seventh Night."[13]

The Son of Heaven was very happy and again drank a great cupful [of wine].

A drunken Son of Heaven, his face red as blood, his head wagging, his legs wobbly, his tongue licking [his lips], not caring that three sevens are twenty-one and two sevens are fourteen, stretched himself across the person of Lady Hsü. Lady Overthrower of States hurriedly sat down and arranged herself so that in her lap she could pillow the heels of the feet of the Son of Heaven.[14] Also there was a young girl of seductive beauty, an attendant to Lady Hsü, who, full of spirit, picked a chrysanthemum flower. With a "hee-hee" laugh she walked over behind Lady Hsü and gently stuck it on the head of the Son of Heaven, turning him into the form of a drunken Son of Heaven intoxicated with flowers.[15]

The whole passage is filled with mockery and ridicule. Initially the emperor and his ministers are compared to sleeping immortals. The absurdity of this, however, is borne out by what follows, when the emperor is shown as one immersed in the pursuit of sensual pleasures. Surrounded by his women he soon becomes thoroughly inebriated. He is utterly vain as he places himself and his two ladies in front of the mirror, seeking the admiration of all present. In the end his appearance is so foolish that he is even mocked by one of his own servants.

The maid next comments on the transitory nature of life. She describes a magnificent theatrical stage constructed by the former emperor and tells how lavish the performances there were. Yet upon visiting the area only recently she saw that the great stage and its buildings were now deserted and falling into ruin. Not only is the gay and sensuous life of the court ridiculous to an observer but it is transitory and of little lasting value or meaning. We see how the maid's speech on one hand satirizes the emperor and on the other hand supports the Buddhist theme of the novel.

Finally, the maid tells of a Taoist priest who held the view that what the Son of Heaven really enjoyed were paintings of people and landscapes. And so the Taoist gave the emperor a painting of Black Horse Mountain. Here it is implied that the emperor prefers the world of the painting to the real world, and the final irony of it all is that the painting turns out to be one of the tomb of the First Emperor of Ch'in, a symbol again of the transitory nature of

human life and strivings. By using the image of the painting Tung
Yüeh raises the question of reality and appearance, a question
implied by the dream itself but also reiterated frequently throughout the novel.

### B. *The imperial examination system*

The passage which most forcefully voices his satire of the examination system is found in Chapter 4. Monkey forces his way into
the Green, Green World, finds himself in the Tower of Myriad Mirrors, and after conversing with an old friend from the earlier novel
who appears in one of the mirrors, decides to investigate the mirrors further. The first one he looks into reveals a scene immediately
following the announcement of successful candidates in a government examination.

In the mirror he [Monkey] saw a man putting up an announcement list-
ing successful examination candidates. The text of the announcement
went:

> In the first place is the Imperially
> Examined Budding Talent (*T'ing-tui hsiu-ts'ai*)
> Liu Ch'un (Willow Spring).[16]
> In the second place in the Imperially
> Examined Budding Talent Wu Yu (Non-being).
> In the third place is the Imperially
> Examined Budding Talent Kao Wei-ming (High
> [but] Not-yet Enlightened).[17]

What follows is first a description of the way in which the examination candidates and their friends react to the announcement.
Unsuccessful candidates react like this:

In a short while there were thousands and tens of thousands of people
crowding and pressing together, shouting and calling out, all coming to
read the announcement. At first there was just the sound of a confusion of
high-pitched voices. This was followed by the sound of wailing and weep-
ing. And this was followed by the sound of angry cursing. In a little while
the mass of people dispersed with everyone going his own way. One sat
stupidly on the rocks. One went and smashed to pieces his tile ink slab of
Mandarin duck design. One with hair like hemp was beaten and chased by
parents and teachers. One, after opening his personal case, took out a lute
decorated with jade, burned it, and then cried miserably for a time. One
pulled out a double-edged sword from the headpiece of his bed, wanting to

commit suicide, only to have a girl snatch it away from him. One, with head low in inane thought, read over his own examination answers three times. One, with a hearty laugh, slapped the table and shouted, "It's fate, fate, fate!" One hung his head down and spat out red blood. There were several older men who spent some money for wine to help one fellow dispel his sorrow. One, reciting poetry by himself, suddenly recited a line and then wildly kicked the stones with his feet. One would not allow his young servant to report the news that his name was not on the list. One outwardly feigned a sorrowful disposition but inwardly revealed a pleased disposition, as if to say he was one who should have succeeded. One was truly sad and truly angry but forced himself to show a happy countenance and smiling face.[18]

These unsuccessful candidates are now contrasted with the fortunate ones who passed the examination.

There was a group of men whose names did appear on the list. Some of these changed into new clothes and new shoes. Some forced themselves to show an unsmiling face. Some wrote words on walls. Some looked at their own examination answers, read them a thousand times, then folded them in their sleeves and went out. Some grieved for their friends. Some intentionally remarked that the examination officials were not up to standard. Some compelled others to read the published announcement, and although these may not in their hearts have wished to do so, they forced themselves to read to the end. Some engaged in animated, high-flown talk saying that this year's examinations were most fair. Some stated that on New Year's Eve all had been revealed in a dream. Some said that the written answers this time were unsatisfactory.[19]

Here Tung draws the scene with great care. He shows remarkable understanding of the psychological factors involved in varying reactions to the examination results. What is stressed is the inordinate importance attached to this announcement. Yet, so far the cutting edge of Tung's satire has not been felt. This comes in a description not of the candidates but of the winning essay.

It was not long before someone had copied passages submitted by the man who placed first and in a wine shop was wagging his head and reading them aloud. By his side was a youth who asked, "Why is this essay so short?" The one reading aloud answered, "The essay was long. I just chose the best lines to copy down. Hurry over and look at them with me. You can learn some standard patterns and then next year you may be successful." Then the two began reading with clear voices. The text read:

The unfinished business to be taken up
Is the promotion of human relationships.
The true view of the (*Ta-*) *hsüeh* (*Great*
     *Learning*) and the *Chung-(yung)*
     (*Doctrine of the Mean*)
Is the perfect spirit of government.[20]
How is this so?
This realm, like chaos, is unattainable.
These principles, like respiration, cannot
     be eliminated.
Thus, the essence of basic mind has not yet
     been divulged,[21]
And the embers of the records on wood and
     bamboo are all of the spirit.[22]
In summary,
The first task of creation
In general cannot hope to reach the *Chung-yung*
     (*Doctrine of the Mean*),[23] and thus
     be passed down,
For the secret fate of ghosts and spirits
Has consisted in gaining the minuteness of
     a small handful.[24]

When in his dream Monkey reads these passages he himself has
to give a hearty laugh. In form they show the pattern of the eight-
legged examination essay. Lines one through four state the theme.
Lines five through seven elaborate the theme. Lines eight and nine
further expand the theme. Finally, lines ten through fourteen conclude the theme. However, although the form is there, the content
is a mixture of high-sounding phrases, possible references to the
classics, and just plain nonsense, all of which is strung together
incongruously. There is a deliberate lack of clarity in these passages
and the reader may take them as a linguistic game in parallelism.
The outcome is that the whole thing seems ridiculous and absurd
and yet is given as the essence of the winning essay. Furthermore, it
is held up for high admiration by one of the characters and is taken
as a model to be followed.

Finally, Tung gives full vent to his contempt for the examination
system. Monkey tells of a conversation he overheard years ago in
heaven between Lao-tzu and the Jade Historian Immortal. Lao-tzu
divided up the history of composition into four periods, each of
which showed that the art had declined over the level of the preceding period. In the final period the art has really been corrupted.

Then the Jade Historian Immortal asked, "How has it been corrupted?'' Lao-tzu answered, ''Alas, there is a group of people without ears and eyes, without tongues and noses, without hands and feet, without heart and lungs, without bones and tendons, without blood and breath, who in name are called those of Budding Talent,[25] but who in one hundred years only make use of one sheet of paper and when their caskets are closed don't even have [an understanding of] two sentences from the books.[26]

The desire for worldly recognition and success fostered by the examination system is merely another form of illusory experience, and this description of the system makes all who participate in it appear ludicrous. The fact that the scene takes place in a mirror serves to raise once again the question of the true and the false, of reality and appearance.

## C. *Men of blind attachment*

In several places Tung Yüeh directs his satire against famous people in Chinese history who are made to appear foolish because of their blind attachment to the physical world. An example is his treatment of Hsiang Yü.[27] Regardless of what evaluation one may choose to make of the historical Hsiang Yü, it is clear that a certain image of him was created first by Szu-ma Ch'ien and then by popular tradition as it developed through the years.[28] He was seen as ambitious and vain and as an opportunist who would stop at nothing in his attempt to satisfy his greed. Tung incorporates this image into his novel. Hsiang Yü is depicted as arrogant and pretentious as he assumes the role of a storyteller and spends a whole night telling of his exploits.

But Tung's satire is not directed at Hsiang Yü's political ambitions so much as at his infatuation with his concubine Beauty Yü (Yü Mei-jen). In Chapter 6 Monkey is in the World of the Ancients and suddenly comes upon Hsiang Yü. Following his mischievous nature Monkey decides to play a trick on the famous Ch'u general and so he disguises himself as Beauty Yü. Then he announces that the real Beauty Yü is in fact Monkey in disguise and moreover is guilty of an act of indecent assault. Hsiang Yü shows himself helplessly gullible.

When Hsiang Yü heard this, he took his sword with his left hand and grasped his lance with his right hand. Giving a great shout, ''Kill him!'' he jumped down from the pavilion. He ran straight to the Flower Shade

Couch, cut off Beauty Yü's head, and then threw it, blood and all, into the
lotus pond. He then spoke to the servant girls, "You aren't allowed to cry!
This was the false empress and she has been killed by me. The true empress
is up in my pavilion."[29]

Here Hsiang Yü is thoroughly duped by Monkey, for without
exercising any critical judgment in the matter at all he accepts Monkey's story and by an impulsive and foolish act kills his own wife.
He is gullible just because of his infatuation. His emotional attachment blinds him and makes it impossible for him to distinguish the
true from the false. Again we see how Tung's satire furthers his
Buddhist theme. Monkey kills Beauty Yü in order to rid Hsiang Yü
of his attachment. This is made clear through an implied pun:
Beauty's surname is homophonous with the word *yü,* meaning
"passion" or "lust."

### D. *Traitors to China*

In Chapter 9, when Monkey enters the World of the Future he is
coerced into serving as a substitute for Yen-lo, King of Hell, for
half a day. When evening court is held, Ch'in Kuei, the notorious
traitor of the Sung dynasty, is brought in. His evil deeds are so
many that a separate book is required to record them all. The trial
proceeds in eight parts and follows a regular pattern. In each part
Monkey first reads from the record. Then he directs questions at
Ch'in relating to matters covered by the reading. Ch'in answers
these but, of course, never to the satisfaction of the court. This is
then followed by the administration of suitable punishments.

The passage is remarkable for its vivid depiction of the eight sets
of punishments inflicted on the traitor. He is pricked with needles.
He is slapped across the mouth. He is dragged onto a *hsiao-tao-
shan* (mountain of small knives) and his blood pours out beneath it.
He is pulverized with a sledgehammer, plunged into the ocean to be
cleansed, has both sets of ribs torn apart and spread out in the form
of two pairs of wings of a dragonfly, and then is beaten with iron
whips. He has a jar of human pus poured down his throat and is
then sawed into many pieces. He has an iron Mount T'ai lowered
on his back. He is turned into a horse and then is beaten and
whipped and made to run fast. Finally, his body is cut up into thin
strips and these are thrown into a roaring furnace.

The treatment of Ch'in assumes special significance as satire when contrasted with the treatment accorded Yüeh Fei. After Ch'in has undergone the eight sets of tortures, the famous Sung general arrives. Entering to the sound of horns and drums, Monkey bows before him and hails him as Master Yüeh (Yüeh Shih-fu). Monkey then says that all along he had known two masters, Lao-tzu and the T'ang Monk. Now he has a third in the person of Yüeh Fei.[30]

Tung makes it clear that Ch'in Kuei is to be taken not only as the leader of Chinese traitors but as the prototype of those who are to come in the future. The passage below expresses the general mood of this episode as well as the larger context of meaning surrounding Ch'in Kuei.

Monkey told the judge to blow him [Ch'in Kuei] back to his true form. Then he once again read from the record:

> Three days passed and again he [Ch'in Kuei] remained behind memorializing and serving as before. But the emperor's intentions had already shifted. Kuei still feared he [the emperor] might change his mind and said, "May Your Majesty further think on this for three days." Three more days passed and a truce was decided upon.

Monkey said, "How could you pass these three days in leisure?" Ch'in Kuei said, "For these three days I, this guilty devil, had no leisure. When I went to the court and saw that the Sung emperor had already decided for peace and that this sweet business could be accomplished, I went out the gate of the court and immediately laid out a feast at home. In the Brass Bird Pavilion I was very drunk for one day celebrating the downfall of the Sung, the support for the Chin, the ascension of Ch'in [Kuei], and the establishment of my enterprise. The next day I held a great banquet at home for officials who in their hearts were named Ch'in.[31] On that day we played the Chin people's music and did the Dance of the Flying Flower Sword. Moreover, not a single thing from the Sung was used nor a single word of the Sung spoken, and so again I got very drunk for a day. On the third day I sat in the Sweep-away Loyalty Book Room and laughed heartily the whole day. By evening I was drunk again."

Monkey said, "These three days you had quite some inclination for wine! Now we still have a few cups of good wine to offer the minister." Then he told two hundred awl devils to carry out a jug of human pus and to pour the pus into Ch'in Kuei's mouth. Monkey gazed toward the heavens and laughed heartily. Then he said, "The empire founded by Sung T'ai-tsu with blood and sweat was happily and joyfully given away by Ch'in Kuei."[32] Ch'in Kuei said, "Today this human pus [makes me] very unhappy. Hey, Master, since there have been many after me who have acted like Ch'in Kuei and quite a few right now who are acting like Ch'in Kuei, why do you just make me alone suffer?"

Monkey said, "Who told you to be the leader of the present-day Ch'in

Kueis and the model for later Ch'in Kueis?'' Then at once he told the
golden talon devils to bring a saw over. Tying up Ch'in Kuei, they cut him
into ten thousand pieces.[33]

The symbolic significance of Ch'in as a traitor is here projected
into the future. It would be hard not to recognize Tung's intention,
for in this way Ch'in stands for all Chinese traitors up to Tung's
own time. The object of the satire thus includes those in late Ming
China who were seen as betraying their country.

This episode supports the novel's Buddhist theme, for it may be
assumed that Ch'in and most other traitors act out of desire for
personal gain, and this is but another form of illusion. Yet its primary significance is best interpreted as a powerful reflection of
Tung's Ming loyalties and an indication of his keen political
awareness.

## E. *The military establishment*

By Chapter 15 Tripitaka now has, in Monkey's dream, given up
his religious calling and become a general. He raises an army and
leads it into battle on the frontier. Prior to battle the Monk-turned-
general takes his place on a platform before his troops. Detailed
instructions are now sent out and these include the following:

The T'ang Monk told [his subordinate general] White Flag to hoist the
officer roll call banner and to pass on the following instructions: "In the
camp the system of water channels and trenches among the hills must be
detailed and comprehensive. If an advisory retainer or a wandering student, dressed strangely and speaking a different dialect, has been let into
the camp, he shall be beheaded." White Flag passed on the instructions as
commanded.

The T'ang Monk gave further orders: "White Flag, you instruct the
officers and men in the camp that those who do not show up for roll call
shall be beheaded. Those who pass back and forth through the palisade
gate shall be beheaded. Those who feign illness shall be beheaded. Those
who look to the left or gaze to the right shall be beheaded. Those who
recommend themselves shall be beheaded. Those who break ranks shall be
beheaded. Those who jump and shout shall be beheaded. Those taking the
name of another or serving as substitutes shall be beheaded. Those engag-
ing in intimate conversations shall be beheaded. Those bringing women
and children along shall be beheaded. Those with wandering thoughts and
reckless ideas shall be beheaded. Those without fierce determination shall
be beheaded. Those who are quarrelsome and have a temper shall be
beheaded."[34]

The rules contained above reflect the severity of army life in Tung's time. There is, of course, distortion here, for the rules are too severe and the whole passage strains toward the ridiculous. This is surely intentional, for the satire lies precisely in this distortion. Tung lived in a time of great unrest. The imperial armies were continually seeking new recruits to fill their ranks as the military threat to the dynasty was felt both internally through the peasant rebellions and externally through Manchu imperial designs. In the end, the dynasty collapsed when the loyalists were unable to cope with this double threat. Tung's sympathies were clearly with the Ming loyalists. Yet, he could not help but be dismayed at the unbearable conditions leading up to the final collapse. His satiric attack on the military establishment reflects his ambivalent sentiments.

## II  *Kinds of Satire*

Gilbert Highet distinguishes three forms of satire: monologue, parody, and narrative satire.[35] Monologue is defined very simply as an extended speech by one person.[36] A satirist may employ monologue either by speaking "in his own person" or by speaking from "behind a mask," that is, through an agent such as a character in a novel or drama. In either case his method is to present his satire to his audience by means of direct verbal expression. Parody is the imitation or mimicking of the language, style, or ideas of what is usually a serious piece of literature or of a literary form.[37] It relies on an implied comparison between the imitation and its subject and makes its subject appear foolish or ridiculous "by infusing it with incongruous ideas, or exaggerating its aesthetic devices."[38] Narrative satire is a broad, more inclusive category in which the satiric effect is achieved either in the telling or in the acting out of a story. Thus, narrative satire includes narrative poetry, fiction, and drama, and what distinguishes it as a type is the way in which the story itself is used for the author's satiric purpose. Highet notes that his categories are not mutually exclusive.[39] At times there may be an overlapping of forms. Some parodies appear in the form of monologues or of narratives. Also, some monologues appear within a narrative framework, and at times a narrative may be presented through a monologue. Still, the basic formal distinctions hold and Highet has used his scheme successfully in a study of the entire body of satire in Western literature.

If we apply Highet's classification to the *Hsi-yu pu,* we find that it contains all three forms. The sweeping-maid episode quoted above represents an example of satiric monologue. An extended speech by one character serves to satirize the imperial system. Insofar as the speech is on behalf of Tung's narrator, and therefore by extension on behalf of Tung himself (since there is no apparent distance between author and narrator), it may be regarded as a kind of masked satiric monologue.

Tung also makes use of a great deal of literary parody. The examination-essay episode quoted above is one example. In both content and style it parodies the eight-legged examination essay. There are at least two other examples. One is Monkey's prayer to departed spirits in Chapter 1,[40] which through its use of florid language and intentional incongruity makes fun of the conventions involved in writing prayers to the deceased. The other is the letter in Chapter 11 written by the caretaker of the thirteen palaces,[41] which by its excessively obsequious tone mocks the formalities of traditional Chinese correspondence.

Most of Tung's satire, however, corresponds to Highet's general category of narrative satire. As Tung tells his story, it is the kinds of characters he creates and the way they act that fulfills his satiric purpose. Much of this is in the nature of caricature. There are caricatures of the emperor, of Hsiang Yü, and of Ch'in Kuei. It is true that in the popular imagination Hsiang Yü and Ch'in Kuei were already regarded unfavorably. Nevertheless, Tung's depiction of them is so exaggerated that even in terms of the tradition what results is caricature.

Highet uses the metaphor of the distorting mirror for narrative satire,[42] and this well describes the *Hsi-yu pu.* The dream itself reflects Chinese life and the reflected image is deliberately distorted. The device of the dream makes this seem natural and acceptable. And in this way Tung can distort as he pleases without fear of incongruity. He ridicules and criticizes aspects of Chinese life so that their objectionable qualities become visible. Moreover, the image of the mirror itself is employed to underline the function suggested by the metaphor.

As in the case of Western satire, Tung mixes his forms. The parody on the examination essay occurs within the larger framework of narrative satire. The maid's monologue includes passages of narrative satire and is itself part of the larger narrative framework of the novel. This mixing of related forms is aesthetically pleasing and serves to strengthen the total satiric effect, for the different forms tend to reinforce each other.

In considering kinds of satire we may also make nonformal distinctions. There are two extremes of tone or attitude here, and in the Western tradition these are referred to as Horatian and Juvenalian satire.[43] In the former the speaker is basically tolerant and makes his presentation in a relaxed, informal, and witty manner. In the latter the speaker is more serious, tends to be filled with moral indignation, and his humor is often harsh and cutting. Highet writes:

There are, then, two main conceptions of the purpose of satire, and two different types of satirist. One likes most people, but thinks they are rather blind and foolish. He tells the truth with a smile, so that he will not repel them but cure them of that ignorance which is their worst fault. Such is Horace. The other type hates most people, or despises them. He believes rascality is triumphant in his world; or he says, with Swift, that though he loves individuals he detests mankind. His aim therefore is not to cure, but to wound, to punish, to destroy. Such is Juvenal.[44]

Often in Western literature writers will mix these two kinds.[45] If we analyze Tung's satire for its tone we find that Tung does just this, for he provides examples which fit the whole range of the Horatian-Juvenalian scale. The satire on the emperor is on the Horatian end and the satire on traitors on the Juvenalian end. The satire on men of blind attachment is closer to the Horatian, that on the military roughly in the middle, and that on the examination system closer to the Juvenalian. Of course, the contrast in tone is most clear at the two extremes. Tung's basic attitudes and fundamental loyalties are revealed here. The emperor is presented as silly and foolish, and although Tung makes fun of him, Tung does not try to destroy him. After all, Tung was a Ming loyalist and supported the emperor as standing in legitimate line of imperial succession. Ch'in Kuei, on the other hand, is treated quite differently. Tung reveals an attitude toward him of intense hatred and disgust. The punishments meted out are horribly grotesque, and Tung seems intent here not on a cure but on destruction. As Highet points out, a close neighbor to this kind of pessimistic satire is pure invective.[46] Yet Tung's attack is not pure invective but satire for it does contain elements of a crude kind of humor.

### III  Social and Political Significance

Lu Hsün early pointed out that Tung's satire was directed at late Ming society. He therefore concluded, even without access to the more recently discovered Ch'ung-chen edition, that the novel must have been written before the change of dynasty. He writes:

Some commentators believed that certain passages in the book referred to the Ching (Ch'ing) dynasty and that this was a satire written after the fall of the house of Ming. Actually the book contains more digs at Ming fashions than laments over the fate of the country, and I suspect it was written before the end of the dynasty.[47]

There are also those who see in the novel indirect references to the conquering Manchus, and some believe the novel contains elements of political allegory. Liu Ta-chieh is one of these.[48] He argues that Tung used Hsiang Yü to stand for the Ming general Wu San-kuei,[49] by whose capitulation to the Manchus the Ming dynasty came to an end. Ch'in Kuei is taken to represent wicked officials, such as Wei Chung-hsien[50] and Hung Ch'eng-ch'ou.[51] Liu also states:

The Green, Green World naturally refers to the Manchus, and therefore the calendar is reversed. The meaning of the Great General, Slayer of the Green, naturally is that the T'ang Monk, who is a man of Han,[52] has to give allegiance to the Ch'ing.[53]

Chapter 10, in which Monkey encounters a foul smell and Hsin the Ancient (Hsin Ku-jen) tells him that it comes from the neighboring Tartars, is seen as a reference to the Manchus.[54] Finally, the whole melancholy scene in Chapter 12 in which Prince Little Moon and the Monk stroll about together and then are entertained, but all amidst much sadness, is seen as representing the sentiments of loyalist Chinese now living under alien rule. Liu sums up his views:

We can know that this book of his [Tung Yüeh's] is written with some particular purpose in mind,[55] and is by no means merely a work of amusement.[56]

More recently Han Chüeh has taken up this position and has carried the allegorical scheme much further.[57] All references to ch'ing (desire) in the novel and its preface are interpreted as covert references to the Ch'ing dynasty. Thus, the religious allegory is taken as, in fact, a political allegory in disguise, and the Buddhist theme which it supports is seen as a device for sustained political commentary. The World of the Ancients is supposed to represent the Ming dynasty. The World of the Future and the Green, Green World thus represent the Ch'ing dynasty. Monkey under the Mackerel's spell stands for the Chinese under Manchu control. The sky-hackers in Chapter 3 are Chinese rebel leaders and their followers. Just as the sky-hackers finally succeed in cracking open the sky only to cause the Heavenly Palace to come sliding down, so also do the rebels cause not just a change in rule but the very collapse of the native Chinese court. Han Chüeh's allegorical interpretation is elaborate and at times ingenious. Interpreted in this way, the whole novel becomes a Ming loyalist political document designed to awaken the Chinese to their real situation and to incite them to overthrow their captors. Like Monkey at the end of the novel, they too are to rise up and slay the monster that has enslaved them.

This interpretation is attractive and continues to command critical support. For example, in a volume of essays on literati fiction and Chinese culture published in Taiwan in 1975, Wang T'o once again reaffirms the position espoused by both Liu Ta-chieh and Han Chüeh.[58] However, these schemes all assume a post-Ming writing of the novel which must be rejected. The dating of the novel around 1640 eliminates the possibility of many but not all possibilities for political allegory. Words sounding like *ch'ing* could stand for the Manchus, since they adopted the name Ch'ing (pure) as early as 1636. It has been observed that people of late Ming times seemed strangely unaware of the impending crisis and dynastic collapse.[59] Could it be that Tung was a notable exception and that here in his novel we find that he is, in fact, providing a subtle and necessarily indirect warning of the impending Manchu takeover?

Recent mainland scholarship accepts the novel as a late Ming work and makes no attempt at full-blown allegorical interpretations. It stresses the view that the novel reveals a kind of patriotic realism and for this it is highly praised. In line with the Marxist approach, Tung is seen to represent the people's point of view. For example, the editors of the 1955 Peking reprint write:

In the chapter "Ch'in Kuei in a hundred lives will have difficulty redeeming himself and the Great Sage gives all his allegiance to the Majestic Prince,"[60] by means of a concealed and indirect artistic method he [Tung Yüeh] expressed the people's thought very well.[61]

It is believed that the true significance of the novel can only be understood in the light of Tung's patriotic motivations, his lifelong Ming loyalist sentiments, and especially his early involvement in political activities. The Peking editors write:

When Tung Yüeh was young he participated in the Fu She (Revival Society) and threw himself into the midst of the people's democratic struggle. After the collapse of the Ming, experiencing the control and oppression of a foreign race, he was extremely depressed in spirit. In order to escape calamity he repeatedly changed his name and even thought of doing away with names and taking Yü Wu-ming (I Without-a-name) as his name. Also from the matter of the burning of his writings we can see that he was one with a feeling for correct principles and a strong people's point of view. Moreover, it was just these ideas which provided his motivation and purpose in writing the *Hsi-yu pu*.[62]

Most important of all, as a representative of the people and as an arch-patriot, it is argued that the novel attacks late Ming degeneracy and corruption. Hsü Fu-ming writes:

He [Tung Yüeh] observed how, when the Manchu court's invasion of the interior of China became more and more insane and wild, and the national situation increasingly approached a crisis, the one in control at the Ming court, the Ch'ung-chen [emperor], was obstinately self-indulgent, and unusually suspicious and jealous, and the groups of great land-lords and great bureaucrats became all the more insatiably greedy, struggled for authority and seized power, attacked the worthy and capable and overthrew each other, scheming only to gain visible leisure and enjoyment and not caring about the safety or danger of the country. It was this rotten group that he attacked in his *Hsi-yu pu*.[63]

The social and political meaning detected by these critics is expressed in the novel's world as satire. It is surely a mistake, however, to adopt only such a limited view, for the novel's satire also supports its Buddhist theme and can only properly be understood in reference to the implied ideal of detachment from the world. Furthermore, the novel is much more than just a work of satire. The satirical elements are merely one part of a world of meaning projected at several levels. Yet, it would also be a mistake to rule out entirely this interpretation. In the choice and treatment of objects of satire Tung is clearly making fun of those things in late Ming life which appeared to him to be foolish, ridiculous, or hateful. An adequate appreciation of the novel must therefore include an understanding of how Tung Yüeh could take a Buddhist story about a dreaming Monkey with all its mythological significance and infuse into it a satirical comment, so that among other things it also became an instrument for social protest.

CHAPTER 9

# Hsi-yu pu *World as Myth (Collective Reflection)*

THERE is a third and final level of the world of the *Hsi-yu pu,* that of the world as myth. Here the extent of the world goes beyond the context of the fictional Westward Journey and also exceeds the scope of one man's satiric vision of society. Monkey is now more than a fictional dreamer and more than the symbol of Tung Yüeh's frustration with what he saw around him. The novel is now no longer taken as simply a study in psychological realism, or even as merely an exercise in social or perhaps political protest. Its world is expanded to become myth, and in it we find a reflection of man's collective experience.

In English the word "myth" is used in a number of different ways. Joseph Campbell writes:

Mythology has been interpreted by the modern intellect as a primitive, fumbling effort to explain the world of nature (Frazer); as a production of poetical fantasy from prehistoric times, misunderstood by succeeding ages (Müller); as a repository of allegorical instruction, to shape the individual to his group (Durkheim); as a group dream, symptomatic of archetypal urges within the depths of the human psyche (Jung); as the traditional vehicle of man's profoundest metaphysical insights (Coomaraswamy); and as God's Revelation to His children (the Church).[1]

The problem is both historical and semantic. Aristotle used the word *mythos* to refer to a story or a plot regardless of whether the story represented an actual happening or not.[2] Later the accepted meaning of myth was narrowed to refer to a single story, usually within a system of stories known as a mythology, and generally handed down by one cultural group.[3] Such stories were used not only to convey certain fundamental ideas about the world and human life but also to socialize members of the group. Myths and rituals went together and served the function of defining the group and the place of individual members in it. By the time of the Enlightenment in the West such stories were no longer believed and myth was therefore commonly understood as referring to that which was opposed to "reality."[4] Wellek and Warren write:

In the seventeenth and eighteenth centuries, the Age of the Enlightenment, the term had commonly a pejorative connotation: a myth was a fiction — scientifically or historically untrue.[5]

Although still frequently used in this way, there has in recent times been a strong reaction against the view that myths and truth are somehow antagonistic. It has become increasingly apparent that since truth may be expressed in many ways, and indeed some truths are bext expressed symbolically, myths may have contained a great deal of truth all along, and should occupy an important place not only in man's history and thought but also in his literature. There has consequently been a revival of interest in myth among literary critics and a group called the "myth critics" has appeared.[6] Northrop Frye, who may be regarded as the leading member of this group, sees the various genres in literature and especially their plot patterns as reflecting basic mythical archetypes. These in turn are associated with the ongoing seasonal cycle of the year. Thus, the meaning of myth here refers not to an ancient, unbelievable story but to the basic, primal patterns of all literature.

Interest in myth has been furthered also by twentieth-century developments in the study of human psychology. Carl Jung suggested that there are two levels of the unconscious, the personal and the collective. At the collective level the human psyche reveals universal, archetypal patterns, and these are expressed in myths.

As our understanding of myth has changed, new meanings have been added. Since one can find in current usage both the old and new meanings, a confusion inevitably centers on this word. Abrams warns that the student should be "alert to the bewildering variety of applications of the term 'myth' in contemporary criticism," and adds that "its uses range all the way from a widely held fallacy ('the myth of progress,' 'the American success myth') to the solidly imagined realm in which a work of fiction is enacted ('Faulkner's myth of Yoknapatawpha County,' 'the mythical world of *Moby*

*Dick*').''[7] Wellek and Warren also refer to the problem when they
state:

> The term is not easy to fix: it points today to an "area of meaning." We
> hear of painters and poets in search of a mythology: we hear of the
> "myth" of progress or of democracy. We hear of "The Return of the
> Myth in World Literature." Yet we also hear that one can't create a myth
> or choose to believe one or will one into being: the book has succeeded the
> myth, and the cosmopolitan city the homogeneous society of the city-
> state.[8]

In view of this wide range of meaning and usage connected with
the word it becomes important to clarify the way it is used here. I
shall accept a definition of myth based on the views of Campbell
and suggested by John F. Priest. Myth is "the expression of man's
total response to his encounter with reality and his subsequent
effort to secure his own existence meaningfully in the face of that
reality."[9]

Thus, the world of the *Hsi-yu pu* when seen most broadly is that
of myth. The novel expresses an understanding of primal truth the
nature and scope of which is such that symbolism is its best form of
expression. As myth the novel is a form of collective reflection. It
assumes a common validity for the truth it contains and it does so
because that which it reflects is common in the life of man.

## I   *The Novel as Monomyth*

The strongest evidence to support the view that the world of *Hsi-
yu pu* is mythical lies in the fact that it fits the pattern of other
myths. Joseph Campbell has studied a great many of these from
different parts of the world and finds that invariably they follow a
common pattern. This he identifies as the monomyth. The basic
pattern of the monomyth is that of a hero who sets out on an
adventure, during which he is initiated and eventually achieves his
goal and from which he finally returns to benefit others.

> A hero ventures forth from the world of common day into a region of
> supernatural wonder: fabulous forces are there encountered and a decisive
> victory is won: the hero comes back from this mysterious adventure with
> the power to bestow boons on his fellow man.[10]

When monomyth is broken down into its basic parts, there is

first the separation or departure of the hero. Invariably in the monomyth there is a break with the common, everyday life. The hero's adventure moves him out of the normal context of his existence and into an unknown realm.

This fateful region of both treasure and danger may be variously represented: as a distant land, a forest, a kingdom underground, beneath the waves, or above the sky, a secret island, lofty mountaintop, or profound dream state; but it is always a place of strangely fluid and polymorphous beings, unimaginable torments, superhuman deeds, and impossible delight.[11]

In the *Hsi-yu pu,* Monkey sets out on a strange adventure which leads him into the dream world of the Mackerel's spell. There he experiences an unknown power over which he has no control. Monkey's movement into the dream, although occurring almost imperceptibly in the novel, is both a separation from reality as he knows it and a departure into an unknown realm.

Campbell refers to a "call to adventure." In the novel this comes from the Mackerel, who, by the allegory connected with his name, stands for desire. Thus, it is desire which calls man into the realm of illusions. After Monkey sets out to beg for alms he first comes upon the New T'ang. Although confused and perplexed by what he sees, he still feels drawn to this strange place, and this is part of the call to adventure.

In some myths there is a refusal of the call. Monkey, it seems, does not really have the option to refuse. The power which moves him into and through the dream is both mysterious and compelling. Monkey is more like Odysseus than Theseus of ancient Greek mythology.[12] His departure from the old world and his entry into the new is the result of the power of the Mackerel working within him.

Normally at this stage in the monomyth the hero encounters a protective figure; however, the pattern may vary.[13] In Monkey's case, a benign power supports him throughout his dream, yet this power does not manifest itself until Chapter 10. When Monkey finds himself trapped in the Tower of Vines and Creepers, his savior is an old man. Significantly this is the standard form of the protective figure in the monomyth.[14]

Monkey enters the spell of the Mackerel and, to use Campbell's words, "crosses the first threshold." This may be taken as the mythical meaning of his entry into the New T'ang. When he comes upon this land, he is confused and makes an unsuccessful attempt to clarify the matter by going to Heaven. When he returns and decides to enter the New T'ang, he must first pass by the guardian of the gate. This is another standard personification in the monomyth. The guardian warns him of the dangers ahead.

Monkey, who had hoped after seeing the Jade Emperor to take out the books of magical words and purple characters and determine clearly if the Great T'ang was true or false, but who now rather was suffering a great insult, could only put himself down on the end of a cloud and return again to the realm of the Great T'ang. Monkey said, "All I can do is just go on in seriousness and see what it is like." So without hesitation he just walked in at the city gate. The soldier who was keeper of the gate said, "By order of the new Son of Heaven all who speak a strange language or wear strange clothes will be seized and beheaded. Little monk, although you are one without family and dwelling, you too must see that you guard your own life.[15]

Monkey is thus warned of the perils ahead. He crosses the threshold and enters the magic realm. Campbell speaks of moving into the "belly of the whale," taking the symbol from Jonah.[16] In the *Hsi-yu pu,* the symbol is not the belly of a whale but the breath of a mackerel. Yet, the similarity of the symbols of water creatures is striking.

The second part of the monomyth is the initiation in the strange land. This invariably involves a series of trials of increasing intensity with a final culmination in the hero achieving the goal of his quest. The nature of the initiation will, of course, vary, depending on the orientation of the myth. In the central Christian myth, for instance, the departure of the hero is signified by his death. His initiation then takes the form of a trip through the underworld, where there is a series of trials with the climax the resurrection of the hero. Many myths center on the theme of the search for a lost lover, either with or without the Oedipal aspect of the nursery trauma. In these instances the series of trials will culminate in a union with the lover or in the variant form of a meeting with the Goddess. If there has been paternal hostility, there may also be an atonement with the Father.

The *Hsi-yu pu* is based on a Buddhist understanding of life and reality, and this fact is reflected in the initiation stage of its myth. I have already shown how Monkey's dream experiences may be organized into four clusters of episodes and how two trends are revealed in the progression through these clusters.[17] Monkey moves more deeply toward the essence of desire and at the same time his involvements become more personal. That is to say, the trial part of the initiation is one in which through various symbols he is made to experience ever more intensely the temptations of human attachment and individual independence and identity.

The testing is brought to its climax at the point of Monkey's enlightenment. Monkey is called from his dream and its meaning is explained to him. He has now achieved the goal of wisdom and this is in fact a form of apotheosis. Possessing knowledge of the illusory nature of his experience, as well as knowledge as to its cause, he has in fact become divine. He has realized the potential Buddha nature within himself.

The third part of the monomyth is the return of the hero. Campbell writes:

> When the hero-quest has been accomplished, through penetration to the source, or through the grace of some male or female, human or animal, personification, the adventurer still must return with his life-transmuting trophy. The full round, the norm of the monomyth, requires that the hero shall now begin the labor of bringing the runes of wisdom, the Golden Fleece, or his sleeping princess, back into the kingdom of humanity, where the boon may redound to the renewing of the community, the nation, the planet, or the ten thousand worlds.[18]

Within the context of the novel, Monkey does not return to the human world as such but to the fictional world of the Westward Journey. However, this is the common, normal world for him and thus corresponds on the reader's level to the human world. When the Master of the Void awakens Monkey, he tells him at once that Tripitaka is hungry. Then, after the explanation of the dream, Monkey is sent back to Tripitaka on a great gust of wind.

Monkey's return fits the pattern of the monomyth, for it is not simply the return of one who has been off somewhere having a private dream. Rather it is the return of one who has undergone enlightenment and is therefore now able to benefit others. There are two pieces of evidence to support this understanding of Monkey's return. The first is his immediate recognition of the Mackerel who has come along disguised as the new disciple.

> Monkey came running along half way up in space and saw a young

monk sitting next to the Master. Monster vapors extended out for a great distance,[19] and so he knew that this was a transformation of the Mackerel Spirit. He pulled his cudgel out from inside his ear and went down swinging it wildly.[20] Suddenly one little monk turned into the dead corpse of a Mackerel from whose mouth there issued forth a red glow. Monkey followed the glow with his eyes....[21]

Thus Monkey saves Tripitaka by his recognition of the monster and his quick action in slaying it. Presumably only Monkey possessed this power of discernment, for neither Tripitaka nor the other disciples seemed aware of the grave danger presented by this new follower. One may well contrast this situation with that at the beginning of the novel. There it was Monkey who was deceived and who lacked wisdom and understanding. Now, however, a great change has taken place and Monkey is the one with the gift of perception and the power to save.

A second piece of evidence follows immediately on the slaying of the Mackerel. Not only does Monkey show himself to possess wisdom for practical action but he is now also wise in Buddhist ways of thought. His conversation with Tripitaka demonstrates this. The T'ang Monk asks how it can be that although Monkey has been away for several days, he and the other disciples have merely experienced the passing of one hour. To this Monkey replies that it is the mind and not time which confuses.

Campbell's pattern of the monomyth is broad in outline and allows for many variations. Yet, to the extent that it represents a common expression of man's universal quest, it reflects an archetypal pattern. Tung's novel fits this pattern and Monkey's experience may be seen to symbolize universal man's response to his encounter with reality and his unceasing efforts to find meaning in it.

## II   *The Buddhist Nature of the Myth*

In order to understand the mythical dimension of the novel's world at more than just the superficial level it is important to realize that this world corresponds not only to the heroic mythical pattern of Campbell's monomyth but specifically to that subgroup within it which is identified with Buddhism. Buddhist myths make up a large category in themselves and show distinctive characteristics.

First, they all take as their model the traditional legend of the great struggle and final enlightenment experienced by Gautama Buddha. This is true both in terms of the sequence of events within the myths themselves as well as in terms of the philosophic and religious world view projected by them.

The original Buddha myth tells us that Gautama was born in northern India, possibly around 560 B.C.[22] His father was a king of the Sakya clan and he grew up in luxury. He was married at the age of sixteen to a neighboring princess. To keep the young prince attached in mind to the pleasures of the world no ugliness was allowed in his sight. Nevertheless, in time he experienced the Four Passing Sights and thus came to know of old age, sickness, death, and the way of withdrawal from the world.[23] These four sights constituted for him the great call to adventure to which he responded. One night when he was twenty-nine years old he made his break with the life of luxury and departed on his great quest for truth. For six years he wandered about learning from the great Hindu masters, practicing asceticism, and disciplining his thought through concentration. This was his period of initiation and trial. Enlightenment finally came one evening near Gaya in northeastern India as he sat beneath a fig tree which has come to be known as the Bo Tree or Tree of Enlightenment. The experience had far-reaching significance, for not only was Gautama himself transformed but the whole of the universe responded, showing the cosmic import of the event. For forty-nine days the Buddha remained under the tree in a state of rapture. Then, overcoming the temptation to ignore the suffering in the world, he went out and began his life of teaching and ministry. He had achieved his goal, had penetrated to the source of reality, and now decided to return to his former world, bringing with him a saving boon for all mankind.

This in brief outline is the original Buddha myth, and it will be noted that it faithfully follows the monomyth through its three stages. It contains the separation, initiation, and return of a hero.

A second distinctive characteristic of Buddhist myths is that they are all informed by a similar world-view. The world-view of the original Buddha myth may very simply be stated in terms of the three concepts of desire, illusion, and enlightenment. Man suffers because he has desire. This desire produces attachments of all kinds and a feeling of need for ego fulfillment. These in turn lead to an illusory existence. The cure may be found through enlightenment.

The *Hsi-yu pu* follows the original Buddha myth very closely and also shares its world-view. The basic sequence of events in Monkey's experience parallels that of the original myth and the same three concepts define its world-view. The Mackerel Spirit stands for desire, and so it is desire that causes Monkey to enter the dream world. The one outstanding fact of the dream is that it is illusory, and at the end when Monkey is called from the dream he is not just awakened but enlightened. I have already shown in the chapter on conceptual materials how the concepts of desire, illusion, and enlightenment support the theme of the novel. Its theme as Buddhist fable is indispensable to its world as Buddhist myth.

Moreover, the metaphor of the dream which is so prominent in the *Hsi-yu pu* is assumed in the original Buddha myth. Indeed, the very name Buddha means "the awakened one" or "the enlightened one." Huston Smith writes:

In the Sanskrit root *budh* denotes both to wake up and to know. Buddha, then means the "Enlightened One" or the "Awakened One." While the rest of the world was wrapped in the womb of sleep, dreaming a dream known as the waking life of mortal man, one man roused himself. Buddhism begins with a man who shook off the daze, the doze, the dream-like inchoateness of ordinary awareness. It begins with a man who woke up.[24]

The relevance of this passage to the *Hsi-yu pu* is clear. At the end of the novel Monkey is also one who has awakened from a dream. Taking the novel as myth, we see his dream as symbolizing the waking life of common man. It is now apparent that Monkey also symbolizes mankind in general. This means that what he experiences is in symbolic form what any man experiences and that desire in the novel stands for human desire in general. Indeed, the dream world permeated by desire is the world of unenlightened man. From this perspective we may also say that Tung Yüeh takes a sympathetic view of Monkey, for he identifies himself and all mankind with his mythical hero.[25]

### III   *The Myth and the Collective Unconscious*

With respect to Carl Jung's view that the collective unconscious is often expressed through myth, it is important first of all to understand the distinction between the psychological and the visionary modes of literature.[26] According to Jung, these are two separate ways of dealing with psychic reality in literature. In the psychological mode the author draws his materials from the realm of human consciousness. That is to say, he creates his literature consciously. He may deal with all sorts of emotional realities, but the process whereby these are translated into the creative work necessarily includes passage through his own consciousness. Speaking of the material of psychological literature, Jung says:

This material is psychically assimilated by the poet, raised from the commonplace to the level of poetic experience, and given an expression which forces the reader to greater clarity and depth of human insight by bringing fully into his consciousness what he ordinarily evades and overlooks or senses only with a feeling of dull discomfort.[27]

It is clear that there is a level at which the world of the *Hsi-yu pu* is defined in terms of the psychological mode, which has been treated earlier in the chapter on the world as dream. Tung had a certain perception of psychological reality, which is in this case that of dream phenomena, and to the extent that his work reflects this conscious understanding it may be said to be a work of psychological realism. Indeed, if one is to take the dream as that of a fictional monkey, then the assumption is that Tung is making use of what Jung calls the psychological mode of literature. The reason for this is simply that the monkey of the novel is an objective creation of Tung's conscious mind. Monkey's dream, therefore, is also such a creation. And if we refer to Monkey's "unconscious" in Freudian terms, still it must always be understood as coming to us through Tung's conscious mind. There is, of course, no psychological phenomenon connected with the fictional monkey, or for that matter any monkey at all, apart from Tung's own conscious creation. Tung Yüeh consciously sought to make his novel universally applicable, and this is most easily seen in the Buddhist nature of the myth. Clearly, he took Buddhist truth to apply universally, and to the extent that his novel embodies this truth, he must have intended it to have universal relevance.

According to Jung there is, however, another mode of artistic creation, and this is what he calls the visionary mode. In this mode psychic reality is transmitted through a work of literature directly from the author's unconscious mind. As it does not pass through his own consciousness he is very likely quite unaware of the nature or fact of this transmission. Jung contrasts the two modes of creation in the following way:

In dealing with the psychological mode of artistic creation, we never need ask ourselves what the material consists of or what it means. But this question forces itself upon us as soon as we come to the visionary mode of creation. We are astonished, taken aback, confused, put on our guard or even disgusted — and we demand commentaries and explanation. We are reminded in nothing of everyday, human life, but rather of dreams, night-time fears and the dark recesses of the mind that we sometimes sense with misgiving. The reading public for the most part repudiates this kind of writing — unless, indeed, it is coarsely sensational — and even the literary critic feels embarrassed by it.[28]

Since the materials presented in the visionary mode come directly from the unconscious, they are often obscure as to their nature and meaning. Such materials are commonly characterized by highly imaginative forms, by that which is absurd and monstrous, by demons and all sorts of creatures from the depths of darkness.

After even the most cursory reading of Tung's novel, one cannot but see in it many examples of the visionary mode. One also soon finds that it is impossible to fit all of its materials into a neat, rational scheme. Schemes for interpreting the novel may usefully be applied. Still, the systematic, rational approach very soon shows its limitation. Jung's suggestion of the visionary mode provides an acceptable reason for this.

Once we accept the fact of the visionary mode, then the question of the specific source of this creation arises. The source is the author's unconscious. This, in turn, leads to the question of the nature of the unconscious, and here we find that the two great psychologists, Freud and Jung, disagree. Freud defined the unconscious in personal terms. Thus visionary literature becomes the symptom of some personal maladjustment or conflict. Jung, on the other hand, divides the unconscious into the personal and the collective unconscious. He does not deny that writers may reflect in their works difficulties stemming from their own personal unconscious, but his view is that this is not necessarily the case. A visionary work may reflect the collective unconscious. That is to say, it may reflect a primordial and collective experience which the writer shares with mankind in general or at least with his own generation.

When we now turn to the *Hsi-yu pu* and examine it on the basis of this theoretical scheme, we may conclude that to the extent that it is visionary literature it reflects the author's unconscious. Insofar as it reflects his unconscious, it either reflects his personal unconscious or the collective unconscious. If we follow Freud and choose the former, then we must assume that Tung Yüeh was a deeply disturbed man personally. Liu Fu takes precisely this position, but without convincing proof. The other possibility is to follow Jung's theory and see in the novel a reflection of the collective unconscious in which Tung shared.

To identify and interpret the collective unconscious in the novel is a precarious undertaking for the nonspecialist, and no attempt will be made here to probe exhaustively into this matter. Nevertheless, since the novel does seem to reflect the collective unconscious in which Tung shared and this is part of the novel's mythical world, I shall venture to suggest two possible ways in which this is expressed. These are first, through the feeling of dubiety pervading the novel, and second, through its mood of iconoclasm.

From the beginning to the end of his dream, Monkey is in varying states of perplexity, confusion, and doubt regarding the reality and meaning of his experience. The prominence of this sense of dubiety is shown by both the frequency and the length of the passages which describe it. Monkey's confusion begins immediately upon his first sight of the New T'ang. It continues on through his experiences in the World of the Ancients, the World of the Future, and the Green, Green World proper. In fact, Monkey is never really free of uncertainty as to what is happening until he is awakened from his dream. Tung conveys this feeling of dubiety at the very beginning of the dream sequence:

> Now it is said that Monkey leaped into the sky. Gazing off to the East and to the West he searched for a place to go to beg for alms. When after a few hours he did not see a single person he became anxious in his mind. He was just about to put himself down on a cloud, turn around and go back the way he had come, when suddenly some ten *li* away he saw a great city surrounded by a moat. He hurried up to have a look and there above the city wall hung a banner of green brocade on which were written several seal characters in brilliant gold: "The Emperor Who Restores the Dynasty, the New Son of Heaven of the Great T'ang, the Thirty-eighth Generation Descendent of T'ai-tsung."[29]
> When Monkey suddenly saw the two characters, "Great T'ang," he was frightened so that cold sweat broke out all over his body, and he thought, "We have been travelling westward, so how is it that we have come to the East? This must be false. Maybe it's some kind of monster at work again. How abominable!"
> Again he turned the matter over in his mind and said, "I've heard of the

revolving theory and how Heaven is turning round and round. It must be that we have travelled to the end of the Western Paradise and have now turned around and come back east again. If it is like this, then there is nothing to fear, for we need only to travel some more before [we shall be back at] the Western Paradise [again]. Perhaps it is true."

Then he thought about it some more and said, "It's not true. It's not true. For if we had travelled past the Western Paradise, as Buddha is compassionate, why didn't he call out to me? Moreover I've seen him several times and he is not one without feeling or short on showing courtesy.[30] So it must be false."

At this time he thought the matter over again and said, "Old Sun himself almost forgot! That year when I was a monster in the Shui-lien Tung (Water Curtain Cave) there was a brother who was called Pi-yi Shih (Azure Suit Messenger). He gave me a copy of the book *K'un-lun pieh-chi* (*Records of K'un-lun*).[31] In it there was a passage which read, 'There was a place called China which in fact was not China but emulated the name of China and so falsely assumed its name." This place must be a country in the West which falsely takes the name of another. So then it's true."

After a little while Monkey involuntarily blurted out, "False! False! False! False! False! If it emulates China then it should only write 'China.' Why then does it write 'Great T'ang?' Moreover my Master always says that it is a brand new world under the Emperor of the Great T'ang and so how could they have known about it to alter the emblem and change the flag here? It is absolutely not true!"

He hesitated for a long time only to find himself even more without a fixed view on the matter.

Monkey stared at the banner determined now to read what followed but again he saw these fourteen (in the original) words, "The Emperor Who Restores the Dynasty, the New Son of Heaven, Thirty-eighth Generation Descendent of T'ai-tsung." Then jumping and shouting and cursing in the air he said, "It's nonsense! Nonsense! Until now it has been no more than twenty years since the Master left the realm of the Great T'ang. How could it possibly be that almost several hundred years have passed. The Master has a body of flesh and blood and although he did go in and out of the caves of the immortals and he did visit P'eng-tao T'ien (P'eng Island Paradise),[32] still he passes his days like an ordinary man. So how could there be such a great discrepancy [in time]? Surely it is false!"

Again he thought for a bit and said, "Still I can't really know. If there were one emperor each month, then in less than four years all thirty-eight emperors would have been replaced. Perhaps it is true."

At this time Monkey had a mass of doubts which he labored in vain to resolve.[33] And so he alighted on the end of a cloud and recited a secret invocation in order to summon the local earth god to ask about the situation.[34]

If we accept the view that the novel is Buddhist myth and that myths reflect the collective unconscious, then we may see Monkey's confusion regarding his dream experience in two ways. First, it symbolizes man's general confusion regarding life. This is, I believe, what T. A. Hsia refers to when he speaks of the "existential malaise" reflected in the novel. Hsia writes:

> In the *Hsi yu chi* Monkey always knows his enemy or guesses what impossible shape his enemy has assumed. But in the *Hsi yu pu* it is the universe that has gone topsy-turvy; the enemy is hidden; he is everywhere and he is nowhere.[35]

Second, Monkey's confusion also symbolizes the confusion felt by many seventeenth-century Chinese. Jung has observed:

> Every period has its bias, its particular prejudice and its psychic ailment. An epoch is like an individual; it has its own limitations of conscious outlook and therefore requires a compensatory adjustment. This is effected by the collective unconscious in that a poet, a seer or a leader allows himself to be guided by the unexpressed desire of his times and shows the way, by word or deed, to the attainment of that which everyone blindly craves and expects — whether this attainment results in good or evil, the healing of an epoch or its destruction.[36]

The seventeenth century was a time of great change for China. Politically there was the increasing weakness and corruption of the emperors and the government in the last years of the Ming, which eventually made possible the Manchu conquest in 1644. Socially, there was the rise of a new urban bourgeois class. Economically, there was the progression through what Balazs has called "the golden century of early Chinese capitalism."[37] Philosophically, there was the mounting criticism of neo-Confucianism. The seventeenth century was a time of increased awareness of and influence from Western thought. Trade with the West was on the increase and the Jesuits, a small but significant group of Western representatives, enjoyed some prominence in the capital. Any period of extensive change like this is likely to result in a certain amount of confusion and perplexity. This feeling of dubiety, which would be dammed up in the collective unconscious like water in a reservoir, is, I believe, reflected in Tung's novel.

There is a second way in which the collective unconscious is revealed, and this is in the novel's iconoclastic mood. Change implies that one thing be eliminated so that another may take its place. I have already shown that the novel is filled with satire. By definition satire, at least in Juvenalian form, is iconoclastic, for it wishes to tear down and destroy that which it despises. Even Horatian satire, by its demand for reform, seeks change. This negative aspect of the satire in the novel may be seen as reflecting a collective dissatisfaction with existing conditions and a desire for change.

There is at least one very powerful iconoclastic image in the novel. This is the image of the missing Ling-hsiao Tien (Palace of Spirit Mist). In the second chapter Monkey goes to Heaven for clarification on the nature of the strange New T'ang he has just seen.

> Monkey became more and more infuriated. He raced straightway to the [Palace of] Spirit Mist to see the Jade Emperor to ask him for clarification. But when he reached Heaven he saw that Heaven's gate was tightly shut. Monkey called out, "Open the gate! Open the gate!" Someone from inside Heaven answered and said, "Such a slave who doesn't know when there is an emergency! Someone has stolen our Palace of Spirit Mist. There is no Heaven to go to anymore."[38]

Monkey is accused of stealing the palace, but in the next chapter we find out what has really happened. A group of sky-hackers has been commissioned to cut a hole in the sky to make it possible for the Monk to go directly to the Jade Emperor to secure a passport for his trip to the Western Paradise. After Monkey leaves the New T'ang we read:

> Monkey had been unable to determine if the New T'ang was true or false, and had seen that for no apparent reason the Master was to be a general. He was both alarmed and terrified, both worried and depressed. So he quickly jumped up and went off to see where the Master was. Suddenly he heard someone talking up in the sky. Anxiously he turned his face upward to have a look, and saw four or five hundred men holding axes and grasping hatchets, swinging the blades around as they moved their arms; all were there hacking at the sky.[39]

The sky-hackers then tell about themselves. The following is their description of the mishap with the palace:

> Today, having received such treatment by Prince Little Moon, all we could do was sharpen our knives and axes. Although we have learned sky-

hacking, still if we gaze upwards for a long time our necks hurt and if we walk in space for a long time our feet get sore. So at noon we all made an effort at hacking and hacked open a crack in the sky. How were we to know we had made a mistake and had hacked open the bottom of the Palace of Spirit Mist, causing the Palace of Spirit Mist to come sliding and tumbling down? In Heaven there was a confused shout, "Seize the thief who stole Heaven!" Also there was great alarm and some bewilderment, and it was quite a while before things settled down.[40]

Two things are noteworthy in connection with this incident. The first is that the sky-hackers are portrayed as common mortals. In other words, common men are shown as chopping away at the sky so as to cause the great palace to collapse and come sliding down. The second point is that Monkey is the one accused of stealing the palace. That is to say, it is Monkey, whom we have seen as representing man in the myth, who is held responsible.

There are many possible ways to interpret this incident. Those favoring a political interpretation may easily see in it a symbolic reference to the peasant uprisings which brought about the collapse of the dynasty. A more attractive interpretation is that here we have a great iconoclastic image. Balazs has shown how the young literati took the position that their enemy was absolutism.[41] It was a time of eccentrics and individualists, and indeed Tung Yüeh took his place among them. It was a time when, if only briefly after the weakening of the Ming and before the imposition of control by the Ch'ing, the underlying mood of China was expressed, when the deep cultural currents of the country surfaced. These were the currents which were at work all along, although imperceptibly, and which were finally to determine in large measure the events of the revolution of the twentieth century.

The world of the *Hsi-yu pu* as myth is to be understood not only through its correspondence as a Buddhist myth with the pattern of the monomyth, but also by the way the collective unconscious of man, and particularly of man in China during the early seventeenth century, is expressed through it.

# Abbreviations

| | |
|---|---|
| *Ch'ien-chi* | Tung Yüeh. *Feng-ts'ao Anch'ien'chi.* |
| CPHYP | Tung Yüeh. *Hsi-yu pu* (Commercial Press ed.). |
| HYC | Wu Ch'eng-en. *Hsi-yu chi.* |
| HYP | Tung Yüeh. *Hsi-yu pu* (Wen-hsüeh Ku-chi K'an-hsing She ed.). |
| NHC | *Nan-hsün chih.* |
| *Shih-chi* | Tung Yüeh. *Feng-ts'ao An shih-chi.* |
| SKHYP | Tung Yüeh. *Hsi-yu pu* (*Shuo-k'u* ed.). |

# Notes and References

## Chapter One

1. Tung Yüeh, "*Feng-ts'ao An ch'ien-chi* tzu-hsü," in *Ch'ien-chi,* p. 1.

2. Ibid.

3. This is his *Nan ch'ien jih-chi.* See below, pp. 35–36.

4. Eight separate gazetteers are given for Nan-hsün, and this is an unusually large number for a locality at the township level. See *Che-chiang ti-fang chih k'ao-lu,* ed. Hung Huan-ch'un (Peking, 1958), pp. 292–93.

5. These are: (1) *Nan-hsün Chen chih,* ed. Fan Lai-keng, with his preface dated 1840, rpt. in *Nan-lin ts'ung-k'an,* ed. Chou Yen-nien (Shanghai: 1936–1939); (2) *Nan-hsün chih,* comp. Chou Ch'ing-yün. I have not seen the latter. However, it is quoted extensively in Liu Fu's study.

6. *Hu-chou Fu chih,* rev. Tsung Yüan-han et al., photo rpt. of 1874 ed. in *Chung-kuo fang-chih ts'ung-shu* (1970).

7. *T'ai Hu pei-k'ao,* comp. Chin Yü-hsiang, photo rpt. of 1750 ed. in *Chung-kuo fang-chih ts'ung-shu* (1970); *Wu Hsien chih,* rev. Wu Hsiu-chih et al., photo rpt. of 1933 ed. in *Chung-kuo fang-chih ts'ung-shu* (1970); and *Su-chou Fu chih,* rev. Li Ming-wan et al., photo rpt. of 1883 ed. in *Chung-kuo fang-chih ts'ung-shu* (1970).

8. "Liu Fu (1891–14 July 1934), teacher, linguist and man of letters. A devoted student of Chinese language and literature, he was an early advocate of the pai-hua (vernacular) movement. His writings proved that he was an able theorist." For this and additional material on Liu Fu, see *Biographical Dictionary of Republican China,* ed. Howard Boorman (New York, 1968), II, 394–95. For the study mentioned, see Liu Fu, "*Hsi-yu pu* tso-che Tung Jo-yü chuan," appended to Tung Yüeh, *Hsi-yu pu* (Peking, 1955). This edition of the *Hsi-yu pu* will hereafter be abbreviated as HYP. Jo-yü was Tung Yüeh's *tzu* (courtesy name). References to Liu Fu's study are given by pagination for the study itself. Liu Fu indicates that the study was completed in Peking on 29 December 1927. See p. 57.

9. Hsü Fu-ming, "Kuan-yü *Hsi-yu pu* tso-che Tung Yüeh te sheng-p'ing," in *Wen-hsüeh yi-ch'an tseng-k'an,* 3rd series (Peking, 1956), pp. 109–18.

10. Another possible translation is "More About the Pilgrimage," which is used by Yang Hsien-yi and Gladys Yang in their translation of Lu

Hsün, *A Brief History of Chinese Fiction,* 2nd ed. (Peking, 1964), p. 228. Liu Ts'un-yan also uses this translation in his *Chinese Popular Fiction in Two London Libraries* (Hong Kong, 1967), p. 94. I prefer my translation because it is closer to the original Chinese in which *pu* literally means "supplement."

11. The *Hsi-yu chi* is widely believed to have been written by Wu Ch'eng-en (1506–1582 or 1583), a native of northern Kiangsu Province. It was probably written around 1570 with the earliest edition appearing in 1592. See Liu Ts'un-yan, *Wu Ch'eng-en: His Life and Career* (Leiden, 1967), pp. 95–97. Numerous partial translations are available, the most popular being Arthur Waley's; see *Monkey,* 1st Evergreen ed. (New York: Grove Press, 1958). For the first volume of a projected four-volume complete English translation, see Anthony C. Yu, trans. and ed., *The Journey to the West* (Chicago, 1977). Yu gives an excellent summary of the current authorship controversy in his introduction; see pp. 16–21.

12. HYP, p. 48. Two forms of pagination are used in this edition. Prefatory materials and chapters are each numbered separately. At the same time all pages, with the exception of the appended study by Liu Fu, are numbered in one sequence. All references to this edition, excepting those to Liu Fu's work, are given by the latter pagination.

13. The English names used here are the ones introduced in Waley's *Monkey.*

14. Yü Ch'u was a Taoist practitioner and storyteller of the Former Han dynasty (206 B.C.–A.D. 25). The bibliographic monograph of the official history of the Former Han lists in the *hsiao-shuo-chia* (storyteller) section a work by him entitled *Yü Ch'u Chou-shuo (Yü Ch'u's Stories of the Chou),* in 943 sections. See *Han Shu,* Po-na ed. (Shanghai, 1930–1937), 30.21a.

15. Liu Fu, p. 23. For the original poem, see Tung Yüeh, *Shih-chi,* 2.4b. The poem is the fourth in the set and not the third, as is mistakenly given by Liu Fu.

16. Tung Yüeh, *Shih-chi,* 2.4b. Monkey enters the Tower of Myriad Mirrors in Chapter 4, experiences the strange lands of its mirrors, and does not return and finally leave the tower until the end of Chapter 10.

17. For a convenient conversion table for dates, see Liu Fu, pp. 58–62.

18. See Liu Ta-chieh, *Chung-kuo wen-hsüeh fa-ta shih* (Taipei, 1962), II, 388.

19. It may merely be coincidental that words sounding like *ch'ing* in the novel are homophonous with the name of the Manchu dynasty. The Ch'ing-ch'ing Shih-chieh (Green, Green World) may be part of the Buddhist allegory on desire, *ch'ing,* and does not necessarily stand for the Ch'ing dynasty, as Liu Ta-chieh suggests.

20. The Manchus took the dynastic title of Ch'ing in 1636 and were after that clearly an increasingly serious threat to the Ming court. See

Franz Michael, *The Origin of Manchu Rule in China* (Baltimore, 1942), p. 100.

21. Liu Ta-chieh, II, 388.

22. See below, pp. 30–31.

23. See below, pp. 32–33.

24. Both have also published Liu Fu's study on the life of Tung Yüeh. The Peking editors have appended it to their edition and the Taipei editors have published it in a supplementary volume.

25. HYP, p. 7. The Ch'ung-chen reign period (1628–1644) was the last in the Ming dynasty.

26. HYP, p. 18.

27. Ch'ien-ch'ing Yün (Thousand-*ch'ing* Cloud) was on the top of Hu-ch'iu Shan (Tiger Mound Mountain) in Wu County (Wu Hsien) of Kiangsu Province and dates back to 1272, when, according to tradition, a monk named the place from a line in Su Tung-po's (1036–1101) poetry which reads, "Yün shui li ch'ien ch'ing" (Clouds and water beautify a thousand *ch'ing*). A *ch'ing* is equivalent to about 15.13 acres. For this and further information, see *Wu Hsien chih,* 19.26b–27a.

28. See below, pp. 98–102.

29. HYP, p. 40.

30. This view is expressed by the commentator in the Shuo-k'u edition of the novel, which includes the "Replies to Questions." For the comment referred to , see SKHYP, p. 1206.

31. Tung Szu-chang (1586–1627), *Ching-hsiao Chai yi-wen,* rpt. in *Wu-hsing ts'ung-shu,* vol. 162.

32. See below, p. 32.

33. HYP, p. 47.

34. HYP, pp. 35–36.

35. There are two printings of the *Shuo-k'u* available: (1) *Shuo-k'u,* ed. Wang Wen-ju (Shanghai, 1915); (2) *Shuo-k'u* (Taipei, 1963). The latter is a photolithic reprint of the former with one pagination system throughout; for the novel, see vol. II, pp. 1205–40. In this study, reference is always made to the Taipei printing.

36. SKHYP, p. 1205.

37. Liu Ts'un-yan, *Chinese Popular Fiction in Two London Libraries,* p. 94.

38. SKHYP, p. 1206.

39. Layman Chen-k'ung, at the beginning of the "General Explanation," tells us that he wrote notes to the novel. See SKHYP, p. 1207.

40. Sun K'ai-ti, *Chung-kuo t'ung-su hsiao-shuo shu-mu* (Peking, 1932), p. 239.

41. René Wellek and Austin Warren, *Theory of Literature,* 3rd ed. (New York, 1956).

42. Ibid., pp. 140–41.

43. Ibid., p. 241.

44. Ibid., p. 214.

45. James J. Y. Liu, *The Art of Chinese Poetry* (Chicago, 1962), pp. 91–100. See also James J. Y. Liu, *The Poetry of Li Shang-yin* (Chicago, 1969), pp. 199–206.

## Chapter Two

1. See Liu Fu, "*Hsi-yu pu* tso-che Tung Jo-yü chuan," pp. 3–6. For a convenient geneological chart, see p. 6.

2. NHC, 18.4 as cited in Liu Fu, p. 6.

3. NHC, 18.4 as cited in Liu Fu, p. 6.

4. NHC, 18.8 as quoted in Liu Fu, pp. 5–6. The studio named is based on the line "Hsüeh erh shih hsi chih, pu yi yüeh hu?" which is the opening remark by Confucius in the *Analects* and which Legge translates as "Is it not pleasant to learn with a constant perseverance and application?" See James Legge, trans., *Confucian Analects*, rpt. in *The Four Books* (Macao, 1962), 1.1.1.

5. NHC, 18.8 as cited in Liu Fu, p. 5. All ages given are by Western calculation unless otherwise indicated.

6. See *Ming Ch'ing li-k'e chin-shih t'i-ming pei-lu* (Taipei, 1969), p. 733.

7. NHC, 18.9 as cited in Liu Fu, p. 5. Translations of official Ming titles here and in what follows are based on those given in Charles O. Hucker, "An Index to the Terms and Titles in 'Governmental Organization of the Ming Dynasty,' " in *Studies of Governmental Institutions in Chinese History,* ed. John L. Bishop (Cambridge, 1968), pp. 125–51.

8. *Ming Ch'ing li-k'e chin-shih t'i-ming pei-lu,* p. 998.

9. Hsü Fu-ming, "Kuan-yü *Hsi-yu pu* tso-che Tung Yüeh te sheng-p'ing," p. 109.

10. For mention of him in the dynastic history, see *Ming Shih,* Po-na ed. (Shanghai, 1930–1937), 233.7b, 8b.

11. *Ming Ch'ing li-k'e chin-shih t'i-ming pei-lu,* p. 969.

12. Hsü Fu-ming, p. 109.

13. *Ming Ch'ing li-k'e chin-shih t'i-ming pei-lu,* p. 1063.

14. Hsü Fu-ming, p. 110.

15. NHC, 18.23 as quoted in Liu Fu, p. 3.

16. See his "Chi Chang Fu-tzu wen" in *Ch'ien-chi,* 1.13b.

17. Liu Fu, p. 4.

18. Hsü Fu-ming, p. 110, n. 2.

19. NHC, 40.1-5 as quoted in Liu Fu, pp. 4–5. Four works by Tung Szu-chang extant today are listed in the collectanea index *Chung-kuo ts'ung-shu tsung-lu* (Shanghai, 1962), III, 604.

20. *Ming Shih,* 233.8b.

21. NHC, 54.9 as quoted in Liu Fu, p. 3.

22. Yü Yüeh was a native of Te-ch'ing County (Te-ch'ing Hsien) in Hu-chou Prefecture, a neighboring county to Wu-hsing.

23. NHC, 54.8 as quoted in Liu Fu, p. 3. Liu indicates that Wang's *Nan-hsün chih* was an old gazetteer. I have checked the *Che-chiang ti-fang-chih k'ao-lu* but find that it is not listed there.

24. NHC, 47.28 as quoted in Liu Fu, p. 57.

25. For this and more information on Nan-hsün Township, see *Hu-chou Fu chih,* 22.1a–2a. For traditional maps of the area, see *Hu-chou Fu chih,* 1.2a–2b, 1.4a–4b.

26. See *Chung-kuo hsiao-shuo shih-liao,* ed. Kung Ling-ching (Shanghai, 1936), p. 101.

27. NHC, 54.7 as quoted by Liu Fu, p. 7. Here the NHC is quoting from the *Ying-hsü Kuan shih-hua.* The Ying-hsü Kuan was the name of Chang Chien's (1768–1850) studio and presumably this work was by him. Chang was a descendent of Tung's. See below, p. 37.

28. See *Shih-chi,* 1.9b, where two quatrains are given which together with notes supply this information. Wen-ku was the style *(hao)* of Monk Kuang Yin.

29. The books of Tsou and Lu, that is, of Mencius and Confucius. Mencius was born in the State of Tsou and Confucius in the State of Lu.

30. See "Chao Ch'ang-wen Hsien-sheng cha-hsing-ts'ao hsü" in *Ch'ien-chi,* 1.1a. Nan Shan is usually used as a symbol for longevity.

31. *Ch'ien-chi,* 1.1a.

32. Quoted in *Chung-kuo hsiao-shuo shih-liao,* p. 101.

33. See the note which goes with the regulated verse "Yüeh Hsü Yu-chieh *Mi-yu T'ang chi* kan shu" in *Shih-chi,* 5.8a. Hsü Ch'ih, whose courtesy name was Yü-shih, earned his *chin-shih* during the Ch'ung-chen reign and served as *Che-chiang t'i-hsüeh fu-shih* (Surveillance Vice Commissioner of the Chekiang Education Intendant Circuit).

34. Hsü Fu-ming, p. 112. Hsü does not give his source for this information.

35. Hsü Fu-ming takes this woman to have been Tung Yüeh's father's wife and thus technically Tung Yüeh's mother, although not actually the woman who gave birth to him (not his *sheng-mu*). Hsü suggests that the woman who bore Tung died in 1627. See Hsü Fu-ming, p. 110, n. 2.

36. See "Wu Yü-san kao hsü," in *Ch'ien-chi,* 2.8a.

37. "Chi Chang Fu-tzu wen," in *Ch'ien-chi,* 1.13a–14b.

38. "Chi Hsi-ming Hsien-sheng wen," in *Ch'ien-chi,* 1.11a–11b, and "Ye yü Chung-hsiao-miao wei Hsi-ming Hsien-sheng ch'i szu shu," in *Ch'ien-chi,* 1.12a–13a.

39. The dates of these burnings are given in *"Feng-ts'ao An shih-chi* tzu-hsü" in *Shih-chi,* 1b–2a.

40. The wording here is: "fen ... shih-yü-nien ying-chih chih wen." Liu Fu, p. 8, feels that since the *shih-yü-nien* cannot mean "of the last more than ten years," for the burning took place two years after the beginning of the new dynasty and Tung certainly was not writing these essays at such a late date, therefore the words must mean "more than ten years

ago." I suggest rather that the words simply mean "burned . . . more than ten years of examination style essays" (that is, written over a period of more than ten years).

41. Liu Fu, p. 31.

42. NHC, 18.24 as quoted in Liu Fu, p. 33.

43. See *Chung-kuo hsiao-shuo shih-liao,* p. 102.

44. I take this to be the Deer Mountain (Lu Shan) in Wu County of Kiangsu Province not far from the eastern shore of Lake T'ai. See *Wu Hsien chih,* 19.24b.

45. See the notes to the poem, "Ch'un-jih kan-huai hsien-yün," in *Shih-chi,* 11.12b.

46. See, for instance, the poems "Wen ching," in *Shih-chi,* 5.2a, and "Hsiao-t'ung ting-ming tu-ts'un szu Lu Shan yeh," in *Shih-chi,* 5.9a.

47. Monk Nan-yüeh (1604–1672), whose original name was Li Hung-ch'u and whose courtesy name was T'ui-weng, did not become a monk until after the fall of the Ming dynasty. After that he was commonly known as Chi-ch'i Ta-shih (Grand Master Chi-ch'i). Through the diligent efforts of his followers he was released not long after his arrest.

48. The Ling-yen Monastery was a Ch'an monastery located on Mount Ling-yen. The mountain is about twenty-five *li* southwest of Soochow and is famous in Chinese history for, among other things, its association with the beauty Hsi Shih. During the Spring and Autumn period (722–464 B.C.) Lake T'ai formed part of the boundary between the kingdoms of Wu and Yüeh. It is said that Hsi Shih was sent by the king of Yüeh to seduce the king of Wu, who built a palace for her on this mountain. The monastery was first built during the T'ien-chien period of the Liang dynasty (505–520). For further information on the mountain and monastery see *Wu Hsien chih,* 19.18b–19a and 36.20a–21a.

49. Liu Ch'eng-kan, "Tung Jo-yü shih wen chi pa," in *Shih-chi,* p. 1. See also NHC, 47.27 as quoted in Liu Fu, p. 33.

50. See "Lin-shih shih," in *Ch'ien-chi,* 6.10a–12a.

51. See NHC, 54.9 as quoted in Liu Fu. p. 26.

52. See "*Shih-chi* tzu-hsü," in *Shih-chi,* p. 1.

53. See the note to "Hsien-p'ing Yu Lu-hsiang hui-yung chih k'e t'an-mei chih tso-ke," in *Pao-yün shih-chi,* rpt. in *Wu-hsing ts'ung-shu,* 6.17a.

54. See Tung Yüeh's biography in *Nan-hsün Chen chih,* 7.23b.

55. NHC, 18.24 as quoted by Liu Fu, p. 33. Mount Yao-feng is in Wu County in Kiangsu, southeast of Soochow. See *Wu Hsien chih,* 19.15a.

56. Niu Hsiu, Ku-sheng hsü-pien, photo rpt. of ed. with preface dated 1700 in *Pi-chi hsiao-shuo ta-kuan hsü-pien* (Taipei: Hsin-hsing Shu-chü, 1962), 2.5a.

57. See *Chung-kuo hsiao-shuo shih-liao,* p. 102.

58. I have not been able yet to determine the exact location of Eastern Rocky Torrent (Tung-shih Chien). From the many place names used in the diary it is clear that it was on West Mountain (Hsi Shan). Tung often refers

to "coming to West Mountain" (for example, entries for February 20 and April 4). The West Mountain referred to is certainly the island called West Mountain (the full name being West Tung-t'ing Mountain) in Lake T'ai. He also identifies his location as being by a West Lake (Hsi Hu) as, for example, in the entry for January 17. This I take to be the West Little Lake (Hsi Hsiao Hu), located north of the highest peak on the island, P'iao-miao Peak. There was a West Little Lake Monastery by this lake (Tung mentions this monastery in the entry for April 2). Eastern Rocky Torrent was probably by a stream with a beautiful waterfall near this lake and also probably not very far from the monastery. For more information on West Mountain see *Wu Hsien chih,* 19.1a–6b, under Mount Pao (Pao Shan, an older name for the island), and for more information on West Little Lake Monastery see *Wu Hsien chih,* 36.29a–29b.

59. *Nan-ch'ien jih-chi,* rpt. in *Nan-lin ts'ung-k'an tz'u-chi,* ed. Chou Yen-nien (Shanghai: 1936–1939). Nan-ch'ien was one of Tung's Buddhist names.

60. Actually the diary is divided into two parts. The first is called "Tung-shih Chien jih-chi" (Diary of Eastern Rocky Torrent), has 46 entries (spanning 47 days) and covers January 15 through March 1. The second is called "Pao hsüeh chi" (Diary of Waterfalls and Snow), has 142 entries and covers March 2 through July 21.

61. For the relevant passage see NHC, 18.24 as quoted in Liu Fu, p. 33.

62. Hsü Fu-ming believes that this was a woman by the maiden name of Tu who was the principal wife of Tung's father but not the woman who gave him birth. See Hsü Fu-ming, p. 110, n. 2.

63. I have not yet found the location of Evening Fragrance Monastery (Hsi-hsiang An). The gazetteer simply says "he died at Hsi-hsiang," which is earlier identified merely as "Hsi-hsiang An of Wu." The "Wu" here may refer to Wu County or possibly to Kiangsu Province as a whole for which this is the archaic name.

64. See Liu Fu, pp. 56–57. Liu's sources for these dates are *Ch'ien-chi,* 6.17b, and *Shih-chi,* 6.3b.

65. See Liu Fu, p. 56.

66. Ibid.

67. NHC, 47.27–28 and 31, as quoted in Liu Fu, p. 57.

68. The year in which the preface was written is given by its cyclical designation of *chi-szu,* which in itself is ambiguous, for, of course, a *chi-szu* year occurs every sixty years. Here, however, it must be 1929, for the collectanea itself contains material reprinted from other editions and one at least is dated as late as 1929 (see the edition of *Yüeh-he so-wen chi* dated the eighteenth year of the Republic).

69. See Liu Fu, p. 28. These two collections of three *chüan* each also appear on the NHC list. See nos. 69 and 70, as given in Liu Fu, p. 18.

70. See, for instance, "Chiao-an He-shang Yao-feng yü-lu hsü," in *Feng-ts'ao An hou-chi,* 2.4a, which is dated 1681.

71. The Warring States period was from 480–250 B.C. and the seven states were: Ch'in Ch'u, Yen, Ch'i, Han, Chao, and Wei. For the date of completion see *"Ch'ien-chi* tzu-hsü," in *Ch'ien-chi.*

72. Currently available editions of the *Ch'i-kuo k'ao* include the following: (1) Peking: Chung-hua Shu-chü, 1956; (2) nos. 787–789 of the *Ts'ung-shu chi-ch'eng ch'u-pien;* (3) Taipei: Shih-chieh Shu-chü, 1960 (see under the title *Ch'un-ch'iu hui-yao,* which is a volume containing two works: the one with the name of the title by Yao Wen-ch'ü and the *Ch'i-kuo k'ao).*

73. This is reprinted in the *Mei-shu ts'ung-shu* (Shanghai, 1928–1936; Taipei, 1964).

74. The section called "Fei-yen-hsiang chi" is included in *Ch'ien-chi,* 6.5a–6a, with works completed in 1651.

75. Liu Fu, when writing his study in 1927, was apparently not aware of the existence of this diary.

76. Liu Fu regretted that he did not see this work, which he believed to be similar to a diary and which, on the basis of the nature of quotations from it in the NHC, he believed contained material on Tung's life before he was twenty and after he was sixty years of age. See Liu Fu, p. 17. The *Ts'ung-shu tsung-lu* lists this work in two *chüan* as appearing in the *Yü-shu T'ang ts'ung-shu,* which unfortunately is not now available to me.

77. This work is to be found in the Far Eastern section of the University of Chicago Library.

78. Liu Fu, pp. 8–24.

79. Liu Fu gives examples from the list of incomplete works, works which seem to have appeared in name only, works for which the actual authorship is in question, and works whose content overlaps with that of other works. See pp. 25–26.

80. The five works in the *Szu-k'u ch'üan-shu tsung-mu* are the following, with locations given: (1) *Yi-fa,* in 8 *chüan,* 8.11b; (2) *Ch'i-kuo k'ao,* in 14 *chüan,* 81.5a; (3) *Yün-ch'i ting-lun,* in 1 *chüan,* 105.8b; (4) *T'ien-kuan-yi,* 107.11a; (5) *Han Yao-ke fa,* in 1 *chüan,* 193.14b.

81. See *So-yin-shih-te chin-shu tsung-lu* (Peking, 1932), 1.59a.

82. Chu Yi-tsun, *Ming shih-tsung,* photo rpt. of ed. with preface dated 1705 (Taipei, 1962), 81A, 14b–16a.

83. Hsü Tzu, *Hsiao-tien chi-chuan pu-yi* (Taipei, 1963), p. 1008.

84. Ch'en T'ien, *Ming-shih chi-shih,* rpt. of original ed. of 1897-1911 (Shanghai, 1936), pp. 3263–64.

85. Liu Fu, pp. 24–25.

## Chapter Three

1. Liu Fu, *"Hsi-yu pu* tso-che Tung Jo-yü chuan," p. 29.

2. Ibid. p. 4. Chieh-an was one of the styles (*hao*) used by Tung Szu-chang. Jo-yü was, of course, Tung Yüeh's courtesy name (*tzu*).

3. Liu Fu, pp. 7–8.

4. Ibid., p. 29.

5. Ibid., p. 26.

6. NHC, 54.10, as quoted in Liu Fu, p. 35.

7. Liu Fu, p. 35.

8. See the notes to "Mei-hua ju", *Shih-chi,* 6.3b.

9. Liu Fu, p. 36.

10. For a discussion of these, see Liu Fu, pp. 31–32.

11. Even his plum blossom and milk concoction does not seem so strange when compared with foods eaten by modern organic food cultists. See Zack Hanle and Donald Hendricks, *Cooking with Flowers* (Los Angeles, 1971).

12. See Etienne Balazs, *Political Theory and Administrative Reality in Traditional China* (London, 1965), pp. 7–8. Regarding the difficulties of studying seventeenth-century China, Balazs says, "Every well-known man had, besides his family name, at least three other names: his *ming,* which was only used officially; his *tzu,* frequent in letters; and his *hao,* under which he wrote, and by which he was known among his disciples. In addition, most of them indulged in the habit of changing these three varieties of names several times, and it is not rare to find, particularly among artists and monks, up to a dozen or more names for one and the same person. Thus, in order to recognize references to say one hundred important persons of the period (and of course there were many more than a hundred), it is necessary to be familiar with about a thousand names."

13. *Encyclopaedia Britannica* (1971), XV, 171.

14. James Bunyan Parsons, *Peasant Rebellions of the Late Ming Dynasty* (Tucson, 1970), pp. 90–160.

15. Liu Fu, p. 56.

16. Liu Fu, p. 34. This is the argument used by Shen Teng-ying, who is quoted in the NHC and who indicates that the Fu She reached its peak of activity in 1629–1630. Also Shen says that Tung's name does not appear either in Wu Tseng's *Fu She hsing-shih lu* or in Lu Shih-yi's *Fu She chi-lüeh.* There must be an error in the former reference, however, for the *Fu She hsing-shih lu* was a list of Fu She members compiled by Wu Ying-chi (1594–1645), and its supplement, the *Hsü lu,* was compiled by his grandson Wu Ming-tao. See *Eminent Chinese of the Ch'ing,* ed. Arthur A. Hummel (Washington, 1943), I, 52; and also Hsieh Kuo-chen, *Ming Ch'ing chih chi tang-she yün-tung k'ao* (Taipei, 1967), p. 165. Actually, although the peak of Fu She activity may have been in 1629–1630, its last grand meeting was not held until 1642.

17. Liu Fu, p. 34.

18. Hsü Fu-ming, "Kuan-yü *Hsi-yu pu* tso-che Tung Yüeh te sheng-p'ing," p. 113, n. 1. Hsü here presents evidence in support of his position. He shows that: (1) there are early accounts which say he joined; (2) his friends were members and he wrote on their behalf; and (3) secondary evi-

dence supports the reliability of the early accounts.

19. Liu Fu, p. 32.

20. For further evidence in support of this account see Ch'en Yüan, *Ch'ing-ch'u seng-cheng chi* (Peking, 1962), pp. 49–50.

21. Liu Fu, p. 29.

22. Hsü Fu-ming, p. 116.

23. The poem was written on a painting by Lü Hai-shan entitled "Tung Jo-yü Lou-shuang t'iao-chou yi-hsiang."

24. Liu Fu, p. 2.

25. Hsü Fu-ming, p. 116, n. 1.

26. See Ch'en Yüan, p. 2, for a chart showing the place in line of succession of both Nan-yüeh (given as Chi-ch'i) and Tung Yüeh in the Lin-chi school.

27. Yi-hsüan was a native of Ts'ao-chou in modern Shangtung Province. He died in 866. The name Lin-chi comes from the Lin-chi Academy of Chen-ting Fu (after the Ming it was called Cheng-ting) in modern Hopeh Province where he lived and worked. His biography is included in the *Sung Kao-seng-chuan, chüan* 12.

28. Kenneth Ch'en, *Buddhism in China* (Princeton, 1964), p. 359.

## Chapter Four

1. Patrick Hanan has shown that in terms of fiction the primary distinction is between vernacular fiction on one hand and the classical tale on the other. See Patrick Hanan, "The Early Chinese Short Story: A Critical Theory in Outline," *Harvard Journal of Asiatic Studies,* vol. 27 (1967), p. 172.

2. During the Ming dynasty the emperors first resided in Nanking (1368–1420) and then in Peking (1421–1644). After the move to the northern capital the southern capital was still retained as a secondary capital. See Charles O. Hucker, *The Traditional Chinese State in Ming Times (1368–1644)* Tucson, 1961), p. 3.

3. HYP, p. 48.

4. For example, see Ibid., pp. 75, 82.

5. For example, see Ibid., pp. 74, 75, 82.

6. For example, see Ibid., p. 143, where all three are used.

7. Ibid., p. 74.

8. For example, see Ibid., p. 94.

9. For example, see Ibid., p. 154.

10. For example, see Ibid., pp. 233, 254.

11. For example, see Ibid., p. 128.

12. For example, see Ibid., p. 147.

13. Ibid., p. 143.

14. Hanan, p. 175.

15. Ibid.

16. Ibid., p. 176, and Ian Watt, *The Rise of the Novel* (Berkeley, 1967), pp. 9–34.

17. HYP, pp. 58–60.

18. Ibid., p. 81.

19. Ibid., pp. 194–96.

20. Ibid., pp. 178–93.

21. See *Sung Shih,* Po-na ed. (Shanghai, 1930–1937), 473.4b–26a. For a word-for-word comparison of Tung's passages and the corresponding passages in the *Sung Shih,* see Hegel, "Monkey Meets Mackerel: A Study of the Chinese Novel *Hsi-yu pu,*" pp. 67–68, 79–83.

22. HYP, pp. 83–84.

23. Ibid., pp. 105–106. For its treatment as parody, see below, pp. 113–114.

24. HYP, pp. 135–36.

25. Ibid., p. 201.

26. Ibid., pp. 224–26. For a translation of this letter, see Hegel, pp. 35–36.

27. Ibid., pp. 265–69.

28. Ibid., pp. 276–77.

29. Ibid., pp. 218–21.

30. Ibid., pp. 284–86. For the satire here, see below, pp. 118–119.

31. Ibid., p. 66.

32. Ibid., p. 73.

33. Ibid., p. 103.

34. Ibid., p. 109.

35. Ibid., pp. 125–26.

36. Ibid., p. 128.

37. Ibid., pp. 172–73.

38. These appear at the beginning of each chapter.

39. HYP, p. 115.

40. Ibid., p. 309.

41. Ibid., p. 218. Here and in what follows in this section each figure stands for a line of verse and represents the number of syllables in that line. A new stanza is shown by a slanting line (/).

42. HYP, p. 233.

43. Ibid., pp. 72–73.

44. Ibid., pp. 227–28.

45. Ibid., p. 228.

46. Ibid., p. 47.

47. Ibid., p. 237.

48. Ibid., p. 278.

49. Ibid., p. 289.

50. Ibid., pp. 48–49.

51. Ibid., p. 51.

52. Ibid., p. 201.

53. HYP, pp. 301–307. The Venerable One is also called the Hsü-k'ung Chu-jen (Master of the Void). See HYP, p. 300.

54. HYP, p. 111.

55. Ibid., p. 234.

56. Ibid., pp. 261–62.

57. Ibid., p. 270.

58. Ibid., p. 287.

59. Ibid., pp. 288–89.

60. Ibid., p. 290.

61. Ibid., pp. 237–51.

62. For the origin and development of *t'an-tz'u* see Chao Ching-shen, *T'an-tz'u k'ao-cheng* (Changsha, 1938).

63. Yeh Te-chün, *Sung Yüan Ming chiang-ch'ang wen-hsüeh* (Shanghai, 1953), p. 63.

64. The musical introduction is preceded by a seven-syllable quatrain which is given as a *shih* and is not considered to be a part of the ballad.

65. HYP, pp. 116–22.

66. Other examples of strings of images may be found in other writings by Tung Yüeh. For instance, in a prose piece on dreams he gives us a string of thirty-one images of what clouds appear to be. See "Chao-yang meng-shih hsü," in *Ch'ien-chi,* 2.11b–12a.

67. HYP, p. 83.

68. Ibid., pp. 99–100.

69. The *po-chia-yi* (hundred-family-garment) was a garment for a child made from separate pieces begged from many homes and believed to be instrumental in bringing good luck.

70. The Chinese gives *tuan-ch'ang-se,* and the *tuan-ch'ang hua* is a popular name for the *ch'iu-hai-t'ang,* or *begonia evansiana.* See Ch'en Yung-feng, *Chih-wu-hsüeh tz'u-tien* (Taipei, 1966), pp. 81, 159.

71. The Chinese gives *pi-yi-se.* The *pi-yi-niao* were birds that had only one wing each and thus had to fly in pairs. The image is frequently used to stand for a conjugal pair.

72. The Chinese gives *yen-ch'ing-se,* and here I take the *ch'ing* to mean black rather than green.

73. The Chinese gives *yin-ch'ing-se.* I take the *yin-ch'ing* to be an abbreviation for *yin-yin ch'ing-shou* (silver seal [with] green ribbon). These silver seals tied wtih green ribbons were symbols of high official rank during the Han dynasty.

74. The Chinese gives *shih-lan-se. The shih-lan* was another name for the *pai-ch'ien,* or *cynanchum japonicum,* a plant with pale red and white flowers, the stem of which was commonly used for medicinal purposes. See Chia Tsu-chang and Chia Tsu-shan, *Chung-kuo chih-wu t'u-chien* (Peking, 1955), p. 236.

75. The Chinese gives *lu-hua-se.* The *lu-hua* are common flowering rushes or reeds growing in marsh-lands, the scientific name for which is

*phragmiter communis.* See Ch'en Yung-feng, *Chih-wu-hsüeh tz'u-tien,* p. 164.

76. The five colors are *ch'ing* (green or green-blue), *huang* (yellow), *ch'ih* (red), *pai* (white), and *hei* (black).

77. The Chinese gives *hui-wen-chin-se.* The *hui-wen-shih* is a palindrome, that is, a verse which can be read either forwards or backwards. The practice of stitching brocaded palindromes was popular at times in China, and Su Hui (of the Ch'ien Ch'in, 351–394) is said to have woven one in five colors.

78. The Chinese gives *hsiang-szu-chin-se.* There are two possibilities as to the meaning of *hsiang-szu* here. It may simply mean "to think about" and be the name of a kind of brocade associated with thoughts about another person. Or, it may refer to the *hsiang-szu-tzu,* which is a plant with small white flowers with touches of red on them and with seeds like bright red beans, the scientific name for which is *abrus precatorius.* See Ch'en Yung-feng, *Chih-wu-hsüeh tz'u-tien*, p. 81. The plant appears frequently in Chinese poetry and is associated with thoughts for another person. I have arbitrarily chosen the latter meaning here, suggesting that the brocade resembles the famous red-berried plant.

79. HYP, pp. 53–54.

80. See below, p. 82

81. HYP, p. 307.

82. Ibid., p. 52.

83. Monkey enters this Green, Green World in Chapter 4 and does not leave it until the end of the dream in Chapter 16.

84. HYP, p. 83.

85. Ibid., p. 109.

86. Ibid., p. 235.

87. Ibid., p. 308. Note here the play on words in the sequence of the disciples' names: K'ung, Ch'ing, Neng, Ching. When read together these characters may be translated as, "When empty of *ch'ing* one can be pure."

88. HYP, p. 65.

89. Ibid., p. 110.

90. Ibid., p. 211.

91. Ibid., p. 233.

92. Ibid., p. 264.

93. This has been pointed out by Layman Chen-k'ung in his "General Explanation" to the novel. See SKHYP, p. 1207.

94. Hegel suggests that since the Chinese word for jade, *yü,* is homophonous with a synonym for desire, *yü,* therefore the word for jade must also stand for desire. For example, he takes the second half of the subtitle for Chapter 14, "Maid Kingfisher Cord breaks jade at pool's edge," and says that "jade" here has no literal connection with the chapter's contents. He believes therefore that it must refer to desire, that is to say, the maid breaks desire when she commits suicide. See Hegel, pp.

27–28. The interpretation is rather attractive, for in Chinese literature "jade" is commonly used to refer to parts of a woman's body, especially her arms. By synecdoche jade may come to stand for a woman herself and hence for the object of desire. Thus "breaking jade" may be more than just a euphemism here for committing suicide.

95. C. T. Hsia, *The Classic Chinese Novel* (New York, 1968), p. 115.

96. HYP, pp. 117–18.

## Chapter Five

1. Robert Scholes and Robert Kellogg, *The Nature of Narrative* (New York, 1966), p. 4.

2. Wayne C. Booth, *The Rhetoric of Fiction* (Chicago, 1961), p. 151.

3. For a discussion of this, see Booth's chapter entitled "Control of Distance in Jane Austen's 'Emma,' " Booth, pp. 243–66.

4. There is, for instance, the problem of the conflict between self and society which C. T. Hsia sees in much traditional Chinese fiction. See C. T. Hsia, *The Classic Chinese Novel,* (New York, 1968), pp. 299–321. It might be profitable to examine this conflict in relation to possible distance between authors and narrators. An author, especially an anonymous one, is a private figure and may champion the cause of the individual. However, his narrator is cast in the role of the traditional storyteller and is in every sense a public figure who is expected to uphold the standards and values of society.

5. Booth, p. 155.

6. Hanan, "The Early Chinese Short Story," p. 173.

7. For a discussion of the meaning of the term *pien-wen,* see James J. Y. Liu, *The Chinese Knight-Errant* (Chicago, 1967), pp. 210–11.

8. See John Lyman Bishop, *The Colloquial Short Story in China* (Cambridge, Mass., 1965), pp. 7–10. Also see James J. Y. Liu, *The Chinese Knight-Errant,* p. 211.

9. For a study of these three collections together with a translation of four of the short stories, see Bishop, *The Colloquial Short Story in China.*

10. The *San-yen* were published between 1620 and 1628, probably in Soochow. See Bishop, p. 1. For a recent attempt to untangle the complicated history of the short story, see Patrick Hanan, *The Chinese Short Story* (Cambridge, Mass., 1973).

11. For a study of its antecedents, see Glen Dudbridge, *The Hsi-yu chi* (Cambridge, 1970).

12. Patrick Hanan, "A Landmark of the Chinese Novel," *University of Toronto Quarterly,* vol. 30 (1960–1961), p. 325.

13. Hanan has discussed the problem of genre distinction as related to the short story. In this connection he raises issues also pertinent to the *Hsi-yu pu.* He writes: "Does the short story differ significantly, at all stages of the history of Chinese literature, from the category of works to which we

apply the catchall word 'novel'? If it does differ significantly, are the boundaries always drawn in the right places? In other words, are there short 'novels' hidden among the short stories, or perhaps some long 'stories' among the novels? Is the short story one genre or more?" Hanan, "The Early Chinese Short Story," p. 168.

14. HYP, p. 252.

15. Cyril Birch, "Some Formal Characteristics of the *Hua Pen* Story," *Bulletin of the School of Oriental and African Studies* 17:2 (1955), pp. 350–55.

16. Hanan, "The Early Chinese Short Story," p. 173.

17. HYP, p. 65.

18. The Chinese gives *t'u-ch'i,* which literally means "spits out his breath."

19. HYP, p. 47.

20. Ibid., p. 55.

21. Ibid., p. 71.

22. Hanan, "The Early Chinese Short Story," p. 174.

23. HYP, p. 111.

24. Ibid., p. 287.

25. Booth, p. 20.

26. The term "narrator-agent" is used by Booth. See pp. 153–54. Booth refers to both observers and narrator-agents, the distinction being that narrator-agents "produce some measurable effect on the course of events." In my use of the term I disregard this distinction and understand "agent" to mean "agent of the principal narrator," and not as "agent effecting events."

27. HYP, p. 74. Ch'ing-kuo Fu-jen (Lady Overthrower of States) is a name based upon a common phrase in Chinese which suggests a beautiful woman. She is one who "overthrows cities and states." The allusion is to a poem by Li Yen-nien, a man of the former Han dynasty famous for his musical talent. Tradition says that the beauty he referred to was his own sister.

28. HYP, pp. 87–88.

29. Ibid., p. 48.

30. See Arthur Waley, trans., *Monkey*, pp. 3–4.

31. HYP, p. 62.

32. Wu Ch'eng-en, *Hsi-yu chi* (Hong Kong, 1961), pp. 256–68.

33. For example, see HYP, p. 299.

34. See HYC, p. 71. Here, as in the HYP, Monkey transforms himself into a form with three heads and six arms.

35. See HYP, pp. 162–63.

36. See HYC, pp. 159–60.

37. See HYP, p. 101.

38. See HYC, pp. 147ff.

39. See HYP, p. 289.

40. For the final resolution to the problem created by Monkey's double, see HYC, pp. 672–73.

41. HYP, p. 295.

42. HYP, p. 308.

43. C. T. Hsia and T. A. Hsia, "New Perspectives on Two Ming Novels: *Hsi Yu Chi* and *Hsi Yu Pu,*" in *Wen-lin: Studies in Chinese Humanities,* ed. Chow Tse-tsung (Madison, 1968), pp. 240–41.

44. HYP, pp. 47–48.

45. Ibid., p. 299.

46. Ibid., p. 299.

47. Ibid., p. 254.

48. SKHYP, p. 1239.

## *Chapter Six*

1. Karl Beckson and Arthur Ganz, *A Reader's Guide to Literary Terms* (New York, 1960), p. 59.

2. See Scholes and Kellogg, *The Nature of Narrative,* pp. 11–16.

3. Ibid., p. 14.

4. James J. Y. Liu, *The Art of Chinese Poetry,* p. 127.

5. See above, pp. 59–60.

6. See above, p. 68.

7. The Chinese reads *yi ch'ien-k'un* (one *ch'ien-k'un*). *Ch'ien* is the name of the first hexagram in the *Yi-ching* (*Book of Changes*) and stands for the male element and heaven. *K'un* is the name of the second hexagram and stands for the female element and earth. As a compound the two characters designate the cosmos, which by nature is a duality.

8. HYP, p. 47. There is a variant reading for the last two lines as given in the Hong Kong Commercial Press edition. I translate the variant as "We dare to open blind eyes for the finite world, [when we are] willing to separately establish a source for rivers and mountains." The essential meaning is the same in both versions.

9. HYP, pp. 47–48.

10. Ibid., p. 51.

11. For my translation of the passage containing these images see above, p. 58.

12. HYP, pp. 55–56.

13. See above, p. 61.

14. HYP, p. 260.

15. Ibid., pp. 268–69.

16. Ibid., p. 299. There is a play on words here, for the name Wu-k'ung means "aware of vacuity" and the name Wu-huan means "aware of illusion."

17. The Chinese gives: "tsai Ch'ing-yü ch'i-li," which is literally "in the Mackerel's breath." As I indicated earlier, I take breath here to mean spell.

18. For the story of Monkey's birth on the Hua-kuo Shan (Mountain of Flowers and Fruit), see HYC, p. 3. For a translation of this passage, see Anthony C. Yu, *The Journey of the West,* p. 67.

19. I have been unable to find Hsiao-yüeh Tung (Little Moon Cave) used as a proper name anywhere except in the novel, and assume therefore that the name was created by Tung to correpond with Hsiao-yüeh Wang (Prince Little Moon).

20. K'un-lun Shan (K'un-lun Mountain) is one of the two chief Taoist paradises, the other being P'eng-lai Shan (P'eng-lai Mountain). The K'un-lun Mountain is said to be located in the extreme west of China. At its foot grow the peaches of immortality. This is a place of leisure and happiness and is ruled by Hsi Wang-mu (Royal Mother of the West). See E. T. C. Werner, *A Dictionary of Chinese Mythology* (New York, 1961), p. 234.

21. I have been unable to find Yu-mi Kuo (Land of Darkness and Confusion) used as a proper name anywhere except in the novel and therefore assume that the name is Tung's creation.

22. HYP, pp. 300–301.

23. Ibid., pp. 308–309.

24. Here there is overlapping of material from within the dream with material outside of the dream. The earth god is first summoned by Monkey in his dream. See HYP, p. 69. Now after waking up, Monkey questions the earth god about this and remarkably the earth god responds as if aware of his neglect of responsibility in the dream. There is reflected here the view that dreams are not confined to the limits of subjective psychic experiences.

25. HYP, p. 312. The quotation of the sentence on which the teacher is lecturing reads in Chinese as: "Fan-wei t'ien-ti erh pu-kuo." This appears to be based on the following line from the *Book of Changes:* "Fan-wei t'ien-ti chih hua erh pu-kuo." See *Chou-yi chu-su,* in photo rpt. of 1815 ed. of *Shih-san ching chu-su,* 7.10a–10b. It will be noted that Tung's version omits the two characters *chih hua.* Hegel has pointed this out and suggests that either the omission was intentional, in which case Tung wishes to make an ironic remark at Monkey's expense, or it was not intentional, in which case the line alludes to the one in the *Book of Changes* and is meant as an exhortation to the reader. See Hegel, "Monkey Meets Mackerel: A Study of the Chinese Novel *Hsi-yu pu,*" pp. 69–70. Whether intentional or not, the omission of the characters *chih hua* does not affect the basic meaning of the sentence. The idea of the *hua,* or transformation, of Heaven and earth should be assumed here even if the words are omitted, intentional or not. In either case an allusion is possible. Secondly, the real problem seems to be in the identification of the subject of the sentence. If the subject is Monkey's experience, then as Hegel suggests the remark may be ironic. But then the sentence no longer alludes to the *Book of Changes.* If there is an allusion here, then the subject should be "knowledge," as in the original passage. See Wing-tsit Chan's translation of the passage as

also quoted by Hegel: Wing-tsit Chan, *A Source Book in Chinese Philosophy* (Princeton, 1963), p. 265. I prefer to take the sentence as an allusion. This fits the concept of enlightenment as presented in the novel. It is knowledge of the truth that dispels illusion. Also this fits the view that the last episode reflects the same world-view as the opening poem. Cosmic reality is a unity, and when we have the clarity of vision (that is, knowledge) to see this, then we are not in error.

26. See my discussion of the Buddhist concept of self-enlightenment below, pp. 91–93.

27. Eighteen separate meanings for the character have been identified. See *Chung-wen ta-tz'u-tien* (Taipei, 1962), vol. 13, p. 120.

28. *Li Chi,* in photo rpt. of 1815 ed. of *Shih-san ching chu-su,* 22.4a.

29. Hsü Shen (fl. ca. A.D. 100), *Shuo-wen chieh-tzu,* rpt. of Sung ed. (Taipei, 1960), p. 349.

30. For a discussion of the Four Noble Truths and the Eightfold Path see Huston Smith, *The Religions of Man,* (New York, 1958), pp. 107–19.

31. Fung Yu-lan, *A Short History of Chinese Philosophy* (New York, 1966), p. 244.

32. *Fo-hsüeh ta-tz'u-tien* (Taipei, 1969), III, 1995.

33. Dudbridge, *The Hsi-yu chi,* pp. 167–76.

34. Dudbridge, p. 168.

35. See *Combined Indices to the Authors and Titles of Books and Chapters in Four Collections of Buddhistic Literature* (Taipei, 1966), I, 216 and II, 79. Buddhatrata's Chinese name is Fo-t'o-to-lo.

36. See above, p. 31.

37. *Ta-fang-kuang yüan-chüeh hsiu-to-lo liao-yi-ching* in *Chung-hua ta-tsang-ching,* vol. 24, p. 10199.

38. *Yüan-chüeh ching,* p. 10199.

39. Ibid., p. 10200.

40. In this quotation the Chinese word I have translated as "mind" is *hsin,* which may also be translated as "heart." Waley does translate it this way: "Tripitaka said nothing but only pointed again and again at his own heart." See Waley, trans., *Monkey,* p. 119.

41. HYC, p. 143.

42. There are times when he participates as himself, such as in his conversation with Liu Po-ch'in (HYP, pp. 101–102) and in his fight with the Six Thieves (HYP, pp. 162–63).

43. HYP, p. 213.

44. To show his displeasure.

45. Here I follow the text as it appears in both the CPHYP edition (p. 99) and the SKHYP edition (p. 1229). The text in HYP is unintelligible to me.

46. HYP, pp. 214–15.

47. Presumably this refers to the New T'ang, over which Monkey suffered such mental anguish. See HYP, pp. 65–69.

48. This was the Lü-chu Lou (Green Pearl Tower) of Lü-chu Nü-tzu (Lady Green Pearl) in Chapter 5. See HYP, p. 109.

49. HYP, pp. 301–307.

## Chapter Seven

1. See, for example, the seventeen studies on the novel in *Hsi-yu chi yen-chiu lun-wen chi* (Peking, 1957).

2. See, for example, the commentary by Ch'en Shih-pin in *Hsiu-hsiang Hsi-yu chen-ch'üan,* woodblock ed. (Ts'ui-yün Shan-fang, preface by Yu T'ung dated 1696).

3. See Timothy Richard, trans., *A Mission to Heaven* (Shanghai, 1913). Richard interprets the novel in terms of Christian theology. He suggests that the author, like Saint Paul, may have been a converted Christian. The novel is seen as a romantic history of the rise of Christianity in the midst of Buddhism. What it advocates, he believes, is not Confucianism, or Taoism, or Primitive Buddhism, but rather something superior to all three — Mahayana Christianity.

4. C. T. Hsia and T. A. Hsia, "New Perspectives on Two Ming Novels: *Hsi Yu Chi* and *Hsi Yu Pu,*" pp. 229–39.

5. *Ch'ien-chi,* 2.11b.

6. Ibid., 2.12a.

7. Until unification by the Ch'in dynasty in the third century B.C., China was divided into the Chiu-chou (Nine Provinces). These varied in both name and boundaries through the early periods; however, they were consistently nine in number.

8. The Chinese reads: "Yu jen-chiao er yü-shen." I find this difficult to translate. It appears that *jen-chiao* is a compound to be taken parallel with *yü-shen.* Tentatively I translate these as "humaned horns" or "humanlike horns," and "fished bodies" or "fishlike bodies." Tung might have in mind human beings that grow horns and have fishlike bodies.

9. Tai is another name for the famous T'ai Shan (Mount T'ai) in Shantung, one of the five sacred mountains of China. See Werner, *A Dictionary of Chinese Mythology,* pp. 578–80.

10. This may be an indirect reference to the works which Tung himself burned (see above, p. 33) or possibly to the works burned by Ch'in Shih-huang.

11. *Ch'ien-chi,* 2.12b.

12. Ibid., 2.15a–16a.

13. Ch'en Hsüan-chuang (also pronounced Ch'en Hsüan-tsang) was the name of the monk who in the seventh century took the historical westward journey and later became the hero in the story cycle. His honorific name was T'ang San-tsang.

14. The Chinese reads: "Fu yüeh ching yen." I have translated this as

"punishment was very severe." Here I take the character *yüeh* (exceed) as standing for *yüeh* (halberd). The combination *yüeh-fu* (halberds and battle-axes) is common. Thus the line reads: "Axes and halberds (that is, punishment) was very severe (that is, of the essence of severity)." Hegel has also translated part of this passage and gives for this line: "The axe was more stern than the spirit." See Hegel, "Monkey Meets Mackerel: A Study of the Chinese Novel *Hsi-yu pu*," p. 43. Presumably the meaning intended is that punishment was more severe than the spirit of the occasion demanded.

15. HYP, pp. 9–15.

16. *Chou Li (Rites of Chou),* ann. Cheng Hsüan in *Ts'ung-shu chi-ch'eng, ch'u-pien,* II, 162.

17. Cheng Hsüan (A.D. 127–200) was a Han scholar famous among other things for his extensive annotations and commentaries on the classics.

18. The commentary on which this summary is based is interspersed throughout the text in the edition cited above.

19. A. C. Graham, trans., *The Book of the Lieh-tzu* (London, 1960), p. 66. For the original passage, see *Lieh-tzu,* in *Ts'ung-shu chi-ch'eng, ch'u-pien,* p. 39.

20. *Ch'ien-chi,* 2.15a.

21. C. T. Hsia and T. A. Hsia, "New Perspectives on Two Ming Novels: *Hsi Yu Chi* and *Hsi Yu Pu*," p. 240.

22. Ibid., p. 241.

23. Ibid., p. 242.

24. Ibid., p. 243.

25. Hegel, p. 47.

26. Ibid., pp. 47–48.

27. Ibid., p. 47.

28. It should be pointed out here, however, that according to Hegel's view the beating of the children should take place before the dream begins and thus could not properly be considered a dream symbol.

29. Hegel, pp. 48–49.

30. Ibid., p. 56.

31. Ibid., p. 57.

32. Ibid., p. 58.

33. Ibid., p. 47.

34. Ibid., p. 49.

35. Carl G. Jung, *Modern Man in Search of a Soul* (London, 1933), pp. 12–13.

36. Ibid., p. 135.

### Chapter Eight

1. Abrams, *A Glossary of Literary Terms,* p. 153.

2. Western literary critics have observed the need for an implied stan-

dard and for distortion in effective satire. Northrop Frye writes: "Satire demands at least a token fantasy, a content which the reader recognizes as grotesque, and at least an implicit moral standard, the latter being essential in a militant attitude to experience." Northrop Frye, *Anatomy of Criticism*, p. 224.

3. Gilbert Highet, *The Anatomy of Satire* (Princeton, 1962), p. 24.

4. For a study which treats the various forms satire has taken in history and the beliefs out of which these have arisen, see Robert C. Elliott, *The Power of Satire: Magic Ritual, Art* (Princeton, 1960).

5. For a treatment of satire in Han and pre-Han literature, see David R. Knechtges, "Wit, Humor, and Satire in Early Chinese Literature (to A.D. 220)," *Monumenta Serica,* vol. XXIX (1970–1971), pp. 79–98. Lu Hsün has pointed out that satiric short stories were written in the Tsin dynasty (A.D. 265–419). See Lu Hsün, *Chung-kuo hsiao-shuo-te li-shih pien-ch'ien* (rpt. Hong Kong, 1968), p. 35.

6. For an English translation, see Wu Ching-tzu, *The Scholars,* trans. Yang Hsien-yi and Gladys Yang (Peking, 1957). For an excellent full-length study of satire in the *Ju-lin wai-shih,* see Timothy Chung-tai Wong, "Satire and the Polemics of the Criticism of Chinese Fiction: A Study of the *Ju-lin wai-shih,*" unpublished Ph.D. dissertation, Stanford University, 1975.

7. Here I follow the text of the CPHYP, which reads "Fei-ts'ui Kung" (Emerald Palace). See p. 16.

8. The name Kao-t'ang alludes to the "Kao-t'ang fu" by Sung Yü (third century B.C.), which tells how once when the king was visiting Kao-t'ang he had a dream in which an immortal beauty named Lady of Mount Wu appeared and offered herself to him. Later the Ming dramatist Wang Tao-k'un wrote his well-known *Kao-t'ang meng (Kao-t'ang Dream)* based on this story. The name has come to mean a meeting place for lovers and here presumably is used for a kind of mirror with romantic associations.

9. Lady Hsü (Hsü Fu-jen) appears to be a reference to Hsü Chao-p'ei, concubine of Yüan-ti of the Liang dynasty (reigned 552–555), famous for her affair with the minister Chi Chiang.

10. Here I follow the text of the CPHYP, which reads *san-szu-pai-ke* (three or four hundred). See p. 17.

11. Ch'ang-e is the Chinese Goddess of the Moon. She stole the elixir of immortality from her husband, Hou Yi, and fled to the moon. See E. T. C. Werner, *A Dictionary of Chinese Mythology,* p. 43.

12. The Weaving Maid is the star Vega and the Cowherd is the star Aquila. There is a legend with several versions associated with these. See Werner, *A Dictionary of Chinese Mythology,* pp. 73–74.

13. The Seventh Night is the seventh night of the seventh moon, when the Weaving Maid and the Cowherd enjoy their annual meeting. For a description of this festival, see Wolfram Eberhard, *Chinese Festivals* (New York, 1952), pp. 143–45.

14. The Chinese reads: "Tso-le yi-ke hsüeh-hua jou-t'a," which literally means, "[She] made a snow-flake flesh-couch." I translate this freely as "arranged herself so that in her lap she could...."

15. HYP, pp. 74–76.

16. The *hsiu-ts'ai,* or Budding Talent examination, was one of the most important administered in T'ang times. It consisted of the writing of five essays on state policy. James J. Y. Liu writes: "At the beginning of the dynasty, this was the highest examination, but later, due to its difficulty and the small number of candidates who passed, it was no longer held regularly." See James J. Y. Liu, *The Poetry of Li Shang-yin* (Chicago, 1969), p. 15. It should not be confused with the *hsiu-ts'ai* of Ming times.

17. HYP, p. 103. Note the word-play involved in the literal meanings of the candidates' names. Willow Spring suggests a romantic rather than scholarly disposition.

18. HYP, pp. 103–104.

19. Ibid., pp. 104–105.

20. The common abbreviation for these two works is Hsüeh Yung, not Hsüeh Chung, and hence it may be argued that the two characters here are simply a compound meaning "in learning," and that the two lines should be translated:

> The true view in learning
> Is the perfect spirit of government.

However, since there is a later allusion to the *Chung-yung,* I take the two characters to be a deliberate distortion of the common abbreviation and regard this as part of the satiric effect of the piece.

21. Hegel offers another possible translation for this line: "Thus the semen of human nature and the body have not yet been ejected." See Hegel, "Monkey Meets Mackerel: A Study of the Chinese Novel *Hsi-yu pu,*" p. 36.

22. There is an allusion here to a passage in the *Chung-yung.* Legge translates the relevant portion as follows: "The Master said, 'The government of Wan and Wu is displayed in the records, — the tablets of wood and bamboo.' " See *The Doctrine of the Mean,* trans. James Legge, 20.2.

23. Here *Chung-yung* is regarded as a proper noun, chiefly because of the allusion above. It could, however, be taken to mean simply "that which is common or ordinary."

24. HYP, pp. 105–106.

25. Here I follow the text of the CPHYP, which reads *"hsiu-ts'ai"* (Budding Talent). See p. 34.

26. HYP, p. 107.

27. Another example is Tung's treatment of the first Emperor of Ch'in, who also is frequently mentioned in the dream but never appears in person. Significantly the emperor is placed in the Meng-tung Shih-chieh (World of Dim Vision).

28. For Szu-ma Ch'ien's biography, see *Shih-chi (Records of the His-toriographer)*, 7. For a good example of the later image in popular tradition, see "Han-chiang Wang Ling pien," in *Tun-huang pien-wen* (Taipei, 1969), I, pp. 36–50.

29. HYP, p. 133.

30. Lu Hsün has pointed out the significance of these three masters. He believes Tung here reflects Ming eclecticism. See Lu Hsün, *Chung-kuo hsiao-shuo shih-lüeh* (rpt. Hong Kong, 1967), pp. 183–184.

31. That is, those who supported Ch'in Kuei.

32. Sung T'ai-tsu was the first emperor of the Sung and reigned from 960 to 976.

33. HYP, pp. 188–190.

34. Ibid., pp. 285–86. Here I have followed the punctuation in CPHYP. See pp. 138–39.

35. Highet, pp. 13–14.

36. See Karl Beckson and Arthur Ganz, *A Reader's Guide to Literary Terms* (New York, 1960), p. 127.

37. Critics differ in the way they distinguish the terms parody and burlesque. Highet uses parody as the generic term and regards burlesque as a form of low parody. See Highet, p. 103. M. H. Abrams takes burlesque as the generic term and defines parody as a variety of high burlesque. See M. H. Abrams, *A Glossary of Literary Terms,* p. 18.

38. Highet, p. 13.

39. Ibid., p. 14.

40. HYP, pp. 58–60.

41. Ibid., pp. 224–26.

42. Highet, p. 148.

43. For definitions, see Abrams, *A Glossary of Literary Terms,* pp. 154–55.

44. Highet, p. 235.

45. Highet writes: "But the satirists refuse to be marshalled into two armies, the white and the black. They are willful and independent fellows.... A single author will write one satire as an optimist, and follow it by another of the bitterest pessimism.... In a single book, even in a single page, we can see the multiple emotions of a satirist struggling against one another for mastery; and ultimately it is this ferment of repulsion and attraction, disgust and delight, love and loathing, which is the secret of his misery and of his power." *The Anatomy of Satire,* pp. 237–38.

46. Highet, p. 151. Western critics disagree on the question of whether or not invective is satire. For a view which differs from Highet's, see David Worcester, *The Art of Satire* (1940; rpt. New York, 1960), chap. 2.

47. Lu Hsün, *A Brief History of Chinese Fiction,* trans. Yang Hsien-yi and Gladys Yang, 2nd ed. (Peking, 1964), p. 229.

48. See *Chung-kuo wen-hsüeh fa-ta shih* (Taipei, 1962), II, 388–90.

49. Wu San-kuei (1612–1678) was a Ming general who in 1644 was ordered to defend Peking. He delayed taking action and the capital fell to the rebel Li Tzu-ch'eng. Wu then sought the aid of the Manchus, who took advantage of the situation to effect their conquest of China. See *Eminent Chinese of the Ch'ing Period,* II, 877–80.

50. Wei Chung-hsien (1568–1627) was one of the most powerful eunuchs in Chinese history. He opposed the reform-minded Tung-lin party and weakened the Chinese defense against the Manchus by his persecution of Ming generals. He exercised tremendous power under Emperor Hsi-tsung (reigned 1621–1628). See *Eminent Chinese of the Ch'ing Period,* II, 846–47.

51. Hung Ch'eng-ch'ou (1593–1665) was a Ming general who surrendered to the Manchus in 1642. From then on he served them faithfully, suppressing numerous Ming loyalists. See *Eminent Chinese of the Ch'ing Period,* I, 358–60.

52. That is, a Chinese and not a Manchu.

53. *Chung-kuo wen-hsüeh fa-ta shih,* II, 388.

54. HYP, p. 209.

55. The Chinese reads *yu-wei-erh-wei,* which literally means "is done for the sake of something."

56. *Chung-kuo wen-hsüeh fa-ta shih,* II, 388.

57. See Han Chüeh, *"Hsi-yu pu* ch'uang-tso-te shih-tai pei-ching," *Kuo-li pien-yi-kuan kuan-k'an* 1:3 (June 1972), pp. 193–206.

58. See Wang T'o, "Tui *Hsi-yu pu* te hsin p'ing-chia," in *Wen-jen hsiao-shuo yü Chung-kuo wen-hua* (Taipei, 1975), pp. 195–213.

59. See Nelson I. Wu, "Tung Ch'i-ch'ang (1555–1636): Apathy in Government and Fervor in Art," in *Confucian Personalities* (Stanford, 1962), p. 261.

60. The Chinese reads "Mu-wang" (Majestic Prince), and this is a reference to Yüeh Fei.

61. HYP, p. 5.

62. See the editorial comments prefixed to Liu Fu, *"Hsi-yu pu* tso-che Tung Jo-yü chuan,"* p. 1.

63. Hsü Fu-ming, "Kuan-yü *Hsi-yu pu* tso-che Tung Yüeh te sheng-p'ing," p. 113.

## Chapter Nine

1. Campbell, *The Hero with a Thousand Faces* (Princeton, 1972), p. 382. Also, for three definitions of myth as applied to biblical criticism, see John F. Priest, "Myth and Dream in Hebrew Scripture," in *Myths, Dreams and Religion,* ed. Joseph Campbell (New York, 1970), pp. 49–50.

2. See Frye, *Anatomy of Criticism,* p. 52.

3. For a study of such ancient stories handed down in the Chinese cultural tradition, see Derk Bodde, "Myths of Ancient China," in *Mytholo-*

*gies of the Ancient World,* ed. Samuel Noah Kramer (New York, 1961), pp. 367–408.

4. Mircea Eliade writes: "What exactly is a myth? In the language current during the nineteenth century, a 'myth' meant anything that was opposed to 'reality': the creation of Adam, or the invisible man, no less than the history of the world as described by the Zulus, or the *Theogony* of Hesiod — these were all 'myths.' " Mircea Eliade, "Myths, Dreams, and Mysteries," in *Myth and Symbol,* ed. F. W. Dillistone (London, 1966), p. 35.

5. Wellek and Warren, *Theory of Literature,* pp. 190–91.

6. M. H. Abrams includes the following in this group: Robert Graves, Francis Fergusson, Richard Chase, Philip Wheelwright, Leslie Fiedler, and Northrop Frye. See Abrams, *A Glossary of Literary Terms,* p. 103.

7. Ibid., p. 103.

8. Wellek and Warren, *Theory of Literature,* pp. 191–92.

9. Priest, p. 52.

10. Campbell, p. 30.

11. Ibid., p. 58.

12. Campbell writes: "The hero can go forth of his own volition to accomplish the adventure, as did Theseus when he arrived in his father's city, Athens, and heard the horrible history of the Minotaur; or he may be carried or sent abroad by some benign or malignant agent, as was Odysseus, driven about the Mediterranean by the winds of the angered god, Poseidon." Campbell, p. 58.

13. See Campbell, p. 97.

14. Ibid., p. 69.

15. HYP, pp. 71–72.

16. See Campbell, p. 90.

17. See above, pp. 76 and 83–85.

18. Campbell, p. 193.

19. The Chinese reads: *yao-fen wan-chang,* which is literally translated as, "Monster vapors [extended for] 10,000 *chang.*" A *chang* is ten Chinese feet or 141 inches.

20. The Chinese reads: *mei-t'ou mei-nao,* which is literally "without head [and] without brain," that is, "mindlessly." I have translated this freely as "wildly."

21. HYP, HYP, p. 309.

22. See Smith, *The Religions of Man,* pp. 90–95.

23. The four sights were an old man, a sick man, a corpse, and a monk. See Smith, pp. 91–92.

24. Smith, p. 90.

25. This view may be contrasted with Hegel's view that Tung identifies himself with the Mackerel and thus takes an antagonistic view toward Monkey. See Hegel, "Monkey Meets Mackerel," pp. 64–65.

26. Jung makes this point repeatedly in his chapter "Archetypes of the

Collective Unconscious." See Carl G. Jung, *The Integration of the Personality,* trans. Stanley Dell (New York, 1939), pp. 52–95.

27. Jung, *Modern Man in Search of a Soul,* p. 179.

28. Ibid., p. 182.

29. T'ai-tsung here refers to Emperor T'ai-tsung of the T'ang dynasty, who reigned from 627–650.

30. The Chinese reads: "Pu-shih wu-ch'ing shao-mien chih jen," which is literally, "[He] is not a person without feeling and with little face." The latter is a reference to giving face or showing courtesy.

31. I have been unable to find evidence that the *K'un-lun pieh-chi (Records of K'un-lun)* was an actual book and therefore assume that it is Tung's fictional creation.

32. The P'eng-tao T'ien (P'eng Island Paradise) is one of a large number of Taoist paradises. It is inhabited by immortals who have supernatural powers and live in ease and pleasure. See E. T. C. Werner, *A Dictionary of Chinese Mythology,* p. 372.

33. The Chinese reads: "Yi-t'uan wei p'o, szu-yi k'ung-lao." This is a couplet which literally means, "[His] mass of doubts were not yet resolved, [and all his] thoughts and deliberations [to resolve them] were in vain."

34. HYP, pp. 65–69.

35. C. T. Hsia and T. A. Hsia, "New Perspectives on Two Ming Novels: *Hsi Yu Chi* and *Hsi Yu Pu,*" p. 245.

36. Jung, *Modern Man in Search of a Soul,* pp. 191–92.

37. Balazs, *Political Theory and Administrative Reality in Traditional China,* p. 11.

38. HYP, p. 70.

39. Ibid., pp. 85–86.

40. Ibid., p. 92.

41. Balazs, p. 16.

# Selected Bibliography

## PRIMARY SOURCES

TUNG YÜEH. *Ch'i-kuo k'ao (Study of the Seven States)*. Rpt. in *Ts'ung-shu chi-ch'eng ch'u-pien*. Shanghai, 1935–1937. Nos. 787–789. Rpt. Peking: Chung-hua Shu-chü, 1956. Rpt. Taipei: Shih-chieh Shu-chü, 1960.

_____. *Fei-yen-hsiang fa (Method for Smokeless Incense)*. Rpt. in *Mei-shu ts'ung-shu*. Shanghai, 1928–1936, col. 2, pt. 4.

_____. *Feng-ts'ao An chi (Collection from Abundant Grass Hermitage)*. Postface by Liu Ch'eng-kan dated mid-winter, 1921–1922. Rpt. in *Wu-hsing ts'ung-shu,* vols. 163–170. This collection contains: (1) The *Feng-ts'ao An shih-chi (Collection of Poetry from Abundant· Grass Hermitage);* (2) The *Feng-ts'ao An ch'ien-chi (Former Collection from Abundant Grass Hermitage);* (3) The *Feng-ts'ao An hou-chi (Later Collection from Abundant Grass Hermitage);* (4) The *Pao-yün shih-chi (Collection of Poetry from Pao-yün);* (5) The *Ch'an yüeh-fu (Ch'an Ballads).*

_____. *Hsi-yu pu (Supplement to the Westward Journey)*. Photo rpt. of woodblock ed. with preface by Yi-ju Chü-shih dated 1641. Peking: Wen-hsüeh Ku-chi K'an-hsing She, 1955. Photo rpt. of 1641 ed. Taipei: Shih-chieh Shu-chü, 1958. Photo rpt. of woodblock ed. with preface by T'ien-mu Shan-ch'iao (dated 1793?) in 1963 Taipei ed. of *Shuo-k'u,* vol. II, pp. 1205–40. Rpt. with col. and punc. Wang Yüan-fang. Hongkong: Commercial Press, 1958.

_____. *Nan-ch'ien jih-chi (Diary of Nan-ch'ien)*. Rpt. in *Nan-lin ts'ung-k'an tz'u-chi*. Shanghai, 1936.

## SECONDARY SOURCES

ABRAMS, M. H. *The Mirror and the Lamp.* New York: Oxford University Press, 1953.

BALAZS, ETIENNE. *Political Theory and Administrative Reality in Traditional China.* London: S.O.A.S., University of London, 1965.

BIRCH, CYRIL. "Some Formal Characteristics of the *Hua Pen* Story." *Bulletin of the School of Oriental and African Studies* 17:2 (1955), 346–64.

169

BISHOP, JOHN LYMAN. *The Colloquial Short Story in China: A Study of the San-Yen Collections.* Cambridge: Harvard University Press, 1965.

BOOTH, WAYNE C. *The Rhetoric of Fiction.* Chicago: University of Chicago Press, 1961.

BRANDAUER, FREDERICK P. "A Critical Study of the *Hsi-yu pu.*" Unpublished Ph.D. dissertation. Stanford University, 1973.

_____. "The *Hsi-yu pu* and Its World as Satire." *Journal of the American Oriental Society* 97:3 (July–Sept. 1977), 305–22.

_____. "The *Hsi-yu pu* as an Example of Myth-Making in Chinese Fiction." *Tamkang Review* 6:1 (April 1975), 99–120.

CAMPBELL, JOSEPH. *The Hero with a Thousand Faces.* Paperback ed. Princeton: Princeton University Press, 1972.

CHAO CHING-SHEN. *T'an-tz'u k'ao-cheng (Textual Study of T'an-tz'u).* Changsha: Commercial Press, 1938.

CH'EN, KENNETH. *Buddhism in China.* Princeton: Princeton University Press, 1964.

CH'EN T'IEN (late Ch'ing). *Ming-shih chi-shih.* Rpt. of original ed. Shanghai: Commercial Press, 1936.

CHU YI-TSUN (1629–1709). *Ming shih-tsung.* Photo rpt. of ed. with preface dated 1705. Taipei: Shih-chieh Shu-chü, 1962.

DUDBRIDGE, GLEN. *The Hsi-yu chi: A Study of Antecedents to the Sixteenth-Century Chinese Novel.* Cambridge: University Press, 1970.

EBERHARD, WOLFRAM. *Chinese Festivals.* New York: Henry Shuman, 1952.

ELIADE, MIRCEA. "Myths, Dreams, and Mysteries." In *Myth and Symbol.* Ed. F. W. Dillistone, London: S.P.C.K., 1966.

ELLIOTT, ROBERT C. *The Power of Satire: Magic, Ritual, Art.* Princeton: Princeton University Press, 1960.

*Erh-shih-szu shih (Twenty-four Histories).* Po-na ed. in *Szu-pu ts'ung-k'an* series, Shanghai: Commercial Press, 1930–1937.

FRYE, NORTHROP. *Anatomy of Criticism.* Rpt. New York: Athenium, 1969.

FUNG YU-LAN. *A Short History of Chinese Philosophy.* Ed. Derk Bodde. First paperback ed. New York: The Free Press, 1966.

GRAHAM, A. C., trans. *The Book of the Lieh-tzu.* London: John Murray, 1960.

HAN CHÜEH. "*Hsi-yu pu* ch'uang-tso-te shih-tai pei-ching" (The Background of the Times for the Creation of the *Hsi-yu pu*). *Kuo-li pien-yi-kuan kuan-k'an* 1:3 (June 1972), 193–206.

HANAN, PATRICK. *The Chinese Short Story: Studies in Dating, Authorship, and Composition.* Cambridge: Harvard University Press, 1973.

_____. "The Early Chinese Short Story: A Critical Theory in Outline." *Harvard Journal of Asiatic Studies* 27 (1967), 168–207.

_____. "A Landmark of the Chinese Novel." *University of Toronto Quarterly* 30 (1960–1961), 325–35.

HEGEL, ROBERT E. "Monkey Meets Mackerel: A Study of the Chinese Novel *Hsi-yu pu*." Unpublished M.A. thesis. Columbia University, 1967.

HIGHET, GILBERT. *The Anatomy of Satire*. Princeton: Princeton University Press, 1962.

HSIA, C. T. *The Classic Chinese Novel*. New York: Columbia University Press, 1968.

_____, and HSIA, T. A. "New Perspectives on Two Ming Novels: *Hsi-yu chi* and *Hsi-yu pu*." In *Wen-lin: Studies in the Chinese Humanities*. Ed. Chow Tse-tsung. Madison: University of Wisconsin Press, 1968, pp. 229–45.

*Hsi-yu chi yen-chiu lun-wen chi (Collection of Research Papers on the Hsi-yu chi)*. Peking: Tso-chia Ch'u-pan She, 1957.

HSÜ FU-MING. "Kuan-yü *Hsi-yu pu* tso-che Tung Yüeh te sheng-p'ing" (Concerning the Life of Tung Yüeh, Author of the *Hsi-yu pu*). In *Wen-hsüeh yi-ch'an tseng-k'an*. 3rd series. Peking: Tso-chia Ch'u-pan She, 1956, pp. 109–18.

*Hu-chou Fu chih (Gazetteer for Hu-chou Prefecture)*. Rev. Tsung Yüan-han et al. Ed. Chou Hsüeh-chün and others. Photo rpt. of 1874 ed. in *Chung-kuo fang-chih ts'ung-shu,* ser. 1B, no. 54.

HUCKER, CHARLES O. "An Index to the Terms and Titles in 'Government Organization of the Ming Dynasty.' " In *Studies of Government Institutions in Chinese History*. Ed. John L. Bishop. Cambridge: Harvard University Press, 1968. pp. 125–51.

_____. *The Traditional Chinese State in Ming Times (1368–1644)*. Tucson: University of Arizona Press, 1961.

HUMMEL, ARTHUR A., ed. *Eminent Chinese of the Ch'ing Period*. 2 vols. Washington: United States Government Printing Office, 1943.

JUNG, CARL G. *The Integration of the Personality*. Trans. Stanley Dell, New York: Farrar and Rinehart, 1939.

_____. *Modern Man in Search of a Soul*. Trans. W. S. Dell and Cary Baynes. London: Kegan Paul, Trench, Trubner and Co., 1933.

KNECHTGES, DAVID R. "Wit, Humor, and Satire in Early Chinese Literature (to A.D. 220)." *Monumenta Serica,* XXIX (1970–1971), 79–98.

KUNG LING-CHING, ed. *Chung-kuo hsiao-shuo shih-liao (Materials for Historical Study of Chinese Fiction)*. Shanghai: Chung-hua Shu-chü, 1936, rpt. 1959.

LIU FU. "*Hsi-yu pu* tso-che Tung Jo-yü chuan" (Biography of Tung Jo-yü, Author of the *Hsi-yu pu*). Appended to 1955 Peking ed. of *Hsi-yu pu*.

LIU, JAMES J. Y. *The Art of Chinese Poetry*. Chicago: University of Chicago Press, 1962.

_____. *The Chinese Knight-Errant*. Chicago: University of Chicago Press, 1967.

LIU TA-CHIEH. *Chung-kuo wen-hsüeh fa-ta-shih (History of the Development of Chinese Literature)*. Rpt. Taipei: Chung-hua Shu-chü, 1962.

LIU TSUN-YAN. *Buddhist and Taoist Influences on Chinese Novels*. Vol. I: *The Authorship of the Feng Shen Yen I*. Wiesbaden: Kommissionsverlag Otto Harrassowitz, 1962.

_____. *Chinese Popular Fiction in Two London Libraries*. Hongkong: Lung Men Bookstore, 1967.

_____. *Wu Ch'eng-en: His Life and Career*. Leiden: E. J. Brill, 1967.

LIU WU-CHI. *An Introduction to Chinese Literature*. Bloomington: Indiana University Press, 1966.

LU HSÜN (1881–1936). *A Brief History of Chinese Fiction*. Trans. Yang Hsien-yi and Gladys Yang. 2nd ed. Peking: Foreign Languages Press, 1964.

_____. *Chung-kuo hsiao-shuo shih-lüeh (Brief History of Chinese Fiction)*. Rpt. Hongkong: Hsin-yi Ch'u-pan She, 1967.

_____. *Chung-kuo hsiao-shuo te li-shih pien-ch'ien (Historical Development of Chinese Fiction)*. Rpt. Hongkong: Chin-tai T'u-shu Kung-szu, 1968.

*Nan-hsün Chen chih (Gazetteer for Nan-hsün Township)*. Ed. Fan Lai-keng with his preface dated 1840. Rpt. in *Nan-lin ts'ung-k'an cheng-chi*. Shanghai, 1936.

NIU HSIU (fl. 1687–1693). *Ku-sheng hsü-pien*. 4 chüan. Photo rpt. of ed. with preface to entire *Ku-sheng* dated 1700 in *Pi-chi hsiao-shuo ta-kuan hsü-pien*. Taipei, 1962. Vol. 6, pp. 6418–39.

PARSONS, JAMES BUNYAN. *Peasant Rebellions of the Late Ming Dynasty*. Tucson: University of Arizona Press, 1970.

RICHARD, TIMOTHY, trans. *A Mission to Heaven*. Shanghai: Christian Literature Society, 1913.

SCHOLES, ROBERT, and KELLOGG, ROBERT. *The Nature of Narrative*. New York: Oxford University Press, 1966.

*Shih-san ching chu-su (Thirteen Classics with Commentaries)*. 14 vols. Photo rpt. of 1815 ed. Taipei: Yi-wen Yin-shu Kuan, 1955.

SMITH, HUSTON. *The Religions of Man*. New York: The New American Library, Mentor Books, 3rd printing, 1960.

*Su-chou Fu chih (Gazetteer for Soochow Prefecture)*. Rev. Li Ming-wan et al. Ed. Ma Kuei-fen et al. Photo rpt. of 1883 ed. in *Chung-kuo fang-chih ts'ung-shu*, ser. 1B, no. 5.

SUN K'AI-TI. *Chung-kuo t'ung-su hsiao-shuo shu-mu (Bibliography of Chinese Popular Fiction)*. Peking: Kuo-li Pei-p'ing T'u-shu Kuan, 1932.

*Ta-fang-kuang yüan-chüeh hsiu-to-lo liao-yi-ching*. Photo rpt. in 1962–1965 Taipei ed. of *Chung-hua ta-tsang-ching*, vol. 24, pp. 10197–206.

*T'ai Hu pei-k'ao (Gazetteer for Lake T'ai)*. Ed. Chin Yü-hsiang. Photo rpt. of 1750 ed. in *Chung-kuo fang-chih ts'ung-shu,* ser. 1B, no. 40.

T'AN CHENG-PI. *Chung-kuo hsiao-shuo fa-ta-shih (History of the Development of Chinese Fiction)*. Shanghai: Kuang-ming Shu-chü, 1935.

TS'AO HSÜEH-CH'IN. *Hung-lou meng (Dream of the Red Chamber)*. 2 vols. Singapore: Shih-chieh Shu-chü, n.d.

TUNG SZU-CHANG. *Ching-hsiao Chai yi-wen (Literary Remains from Ching-hsiao Studio)*. *Rpt. in Wu-hsing ts'ung-shu,* vol. 162.

WALEY, ARTHUR, trans. *Monkey*. New York: Grove Press, 1st Evergreen ed., 1958.

WANG T'O. "Tui *Hsi-yu pu* te hsin p'ing-chia" (A New Evaluation of the *Hsi-yu pu*). In *Wen-jen hsiao-shuo yü Chung-kuo wen-hua*. Taipei: Chin-ts'ao Wen-hua Shih-yeh Kung-szu, 1975, pp. 195–213.

WELLEK, RENÉ, and WARREN, AUSTIN. *Theory of Literature*. 3rd ed. New York: Harcourt, Brace and World, 1956.

WONG, TIMOTHY CHUNG-TAI. "Satire and the Polemics of the Criticism of Chinese Fiction: A Study of the *Ju-lin wai-shih*." Unpublished Ph.D. dissertation. Stanford University, 1975.

WORCHESTER, DAVID. *The Art of Satire*. Rpt. New York: Russel and Russel, 1960.

WU CH'ENG-EN. *Hsi-yu chi (Record of the Westward Journey)*. 2 vols. Hong Kong: Commercial Press, 1961.

WU CHING-TZU. *The Scholars*. Trans. Yang Hsien-yi and Gladys Yang. Peking: Foreign Languages Press, 1957.

*Wu Hsien chih (Gazetteer for Wu County)*. Rev. Wu Hsiu-chih et al. Ed. Ts'ao Yün-yüan et al. Photo rpt. of 1933 ed. in *Chung-kuo fang-chih ts'ung-shu,* ser. 1B, no. 18.

WU, NELSON I. "Tung Ch'i-ch'ang (1555–1636): Apathy in Government and Fervor in Art." In *Confucian Personalities*. Ed. Arthur F. Wright and Denis Twichett. Stanford: Stanford University Press, 1962, pp. 260–93.

YEH TE-CHÜN. *Sung Yüan Ming chiang-ch'ang wen-hsüeh (Chantefable Literature of the Sung, Yüan and Ming)*. Shanghai: Shang-tsa Ch'u-pan She, 1953.

YU, ANTHONY C., trans. and ed. *The Journey to the West*. Vol. I, Chicago: University of Chicago Press, 1977.

# Index

Abrams, M. H., 127–28, 165n37, 167m6
Abundant Grass Hermitage (Feng-ts'ao An), 34, 37
Allegory, 23, 59–61, 79–80, 82, 84, 89, 98, 123, 129
Ancient Mirror Carved in Green (Lou-ch'ing Ku-ching), 60
Aristotle, 126

Balazs, Etienne, 139, 141, 151n12
Beauty Yü (Yü Mei-jen), 52, 61–62, 72, 93, 99, 115–16
Beckson, Karl and Ganz, Arthur, 78
Bell for Driving off Mountains (Ch'ü-shan To), 99
Birch, Cyril, 67
Black Horse Mountain, 111
Booth, Wayne, 63–64, 69, 157n26
Buddha, 85–86, 89–91, 133–34, 138
Buddhatrata, 90
Buddhism, and influence on Tung Yüeh's life, 31, 39, 46–49; and interpretation of the *Hsi-yu pu*, 21–22; as therapeutic value for Tung Yüeh, 42
Buddhist fable, 78–79, 83, 93, 134
Budding Talent examination, 112, 164n16
Bull Monster King (Niu-mo Wang), 73

Campbell, Joseph, 126, 128–32, 167n12
Ch'an Buddhism, 34, 38, 47–49, 59
*Ch'an yüeh-fu (Ch'an Ballads)*, 38
Chang Chien, 30, 37, 147n27
Ch'ang-e, 110, 163n11
Chang, Hsien-chung, 45
Chang P'u, 33 45–56
Chang Shih-ch'eng, 30
Changsha, 35
Chao Ch'ang-wen, 31
"Chao-yang meng shih hsü" (Preface

to a History of Dreams of Chao-yang), 95–96
Ch'en Hsüan-tsang, 99, 161n13
Ch'en, Kenneth S., 49
Ch'en T'ien, 39
Chen-tse County (Chen-tse Hsien), 30
Cheng Hsüan, 100–101, 162n17
*Ch'i-kuo k'ao (Study of the Seven States)*, 32, 38–39, 150n71, 150n72
*Ch'ien-chi* (Abbreviation for *Feng-ts'ao An ch'ien-chi, Former Collection from Abundant Grass Hermitage*), 17, 37–38, 95
Ch'ien-ch'ing Yün (Thousand-*ch'ing* Cloud), 21, 145n27
Chih-chiang Pao-yang-sheng (Pao-yang-sheng of Chekiang), 30–31, 32, 34
Ch'in Kuei, 53–54, 84, 99, 101, 105, 108, 116–18, 120–23
Chin Ming-shih, 37
*Chin P'ing Mei (The Golden Lotus)*, 65–66
Ch'in Shih-huang (First Emperor of Ch'in), 99, 111, 164n27
*Ch'ing* (emotions, desire), 59, 61, 80–82, 84, 88–89, 107, 122–23, 144n19
*Ch'ing* (green or green-blue), 60, 84
Ch'ing Fish Spirit. See Mackerel Spirit
*Ching-hsiao Chai yi-wen (Literary Remains from the Ching-hsiao Studio)*, 21
*Ch'ing-yüan* (monkey of desire), 89
*Chou Li (Rites of Chou)*, 21, 100–103
Chu Yi-tsun, 39
*Chü-meng* (dream of fear), 99–100
Chung-kuo Chiu-chou (Nine Provinces of China), 96, 161n7
*Chung-yung (Doctrine of the Mean)*, 114, 164n20, 164n22, 164n23

174